Delights and highlights of Switzerland

1 Château de Villa wine bar in Sierre
Enjoy hundreds of Valais wines in a historic wine bar (see p185)

2 Lavaux vineyard walks and wineries
Explore the ancient terraces overlooking Lake Geneva (see pp98–103)

3 Lausanne restaurants
Dine out in the capital of Swiss gastronomy (see p98)

4 Fête des Vendanges in Neuchâtel
Harvest revelry with fireworks and a colourful parade (see pp84–85)

5 Cycling in the Bündner Herrschaft
Discover the wines of 'Heidiland' on two wheels (see pp111–113)

6 Weinkrone Museum in Hallau
Sip a glass while you discover local winemaking traditions (see p142)

7 Lugano for food and wine south of the Alps
Mediterranean lifestyle surrounded by mountains (see pp113–115)

8 Regional Open Cellar Events
Winemakers throughout Switzerland their doors in late spring (see pp89–91)

All prices are correct at time of going to
press, but are subject to change.

Published 2025 by Académie du Vin Library Ltd
academieduvinlibrary.com
Founders: Steven Spurrier and Simon McMurtrie

Publisher: Hermione Ireland
Series editor: Adam Lechmere
Design: Martin Preston
Maps supplied by Cosmographics
Index: Jenny Sykes
Proofreader: Jenny Sykes
ISBN: 978-1-9170-8469-7
Printed and bound in the EU
© 2025 Académie du Vin Library Ltd

Switzerland

Simon Hardy & Marc Checkley

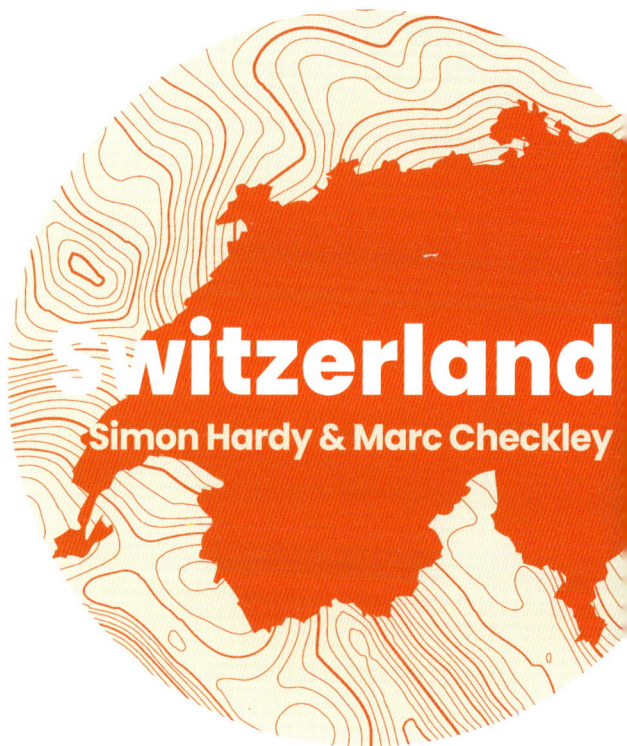

THE SMART TRAVELLER'S
WINE GUIDE

Contents

see p31

see p83

see p118

see p153

View across Lake Geneva from the vineyards of Lavaux

Foreword

I have spent most of my professional life researching the genetics and origins of Swiss grape varieties, yet this book still managed to surprise and impress me. I even picked up a few tips along the way.

The authors have done something quite rare: they've created a guide that's both accurate and insightful, while remaining engaging, practical, authentic and full of character. It's a pleasure to read – not only because of its depth, but because it captures the feel of each place, each wine, each story: what to drink and where to experience it.

I often say that Swiss wine does not exist. Not because it isn't real, but because it's so diverse that it defies easy definition. Diversity doesn't create identity – but it does arouse curiosity. The book taps into this idea beautifully, inviting readers to explore a country where every valley, every slope and every grape tells a unique and different tale.

This is not just a travel guide. It's a book that every wine lover should read – even the locals will learn something from it. Whether you're planning your first visit or you've lived here all your life, it's an inspiring companion that will open your eyes and excite the palate to just how much there is to discover in Swiss wine.

Dr José Vouillamoz
Expert in grape genetics, co-author of *Wine Grapes* (2012),
wine writer & consultant

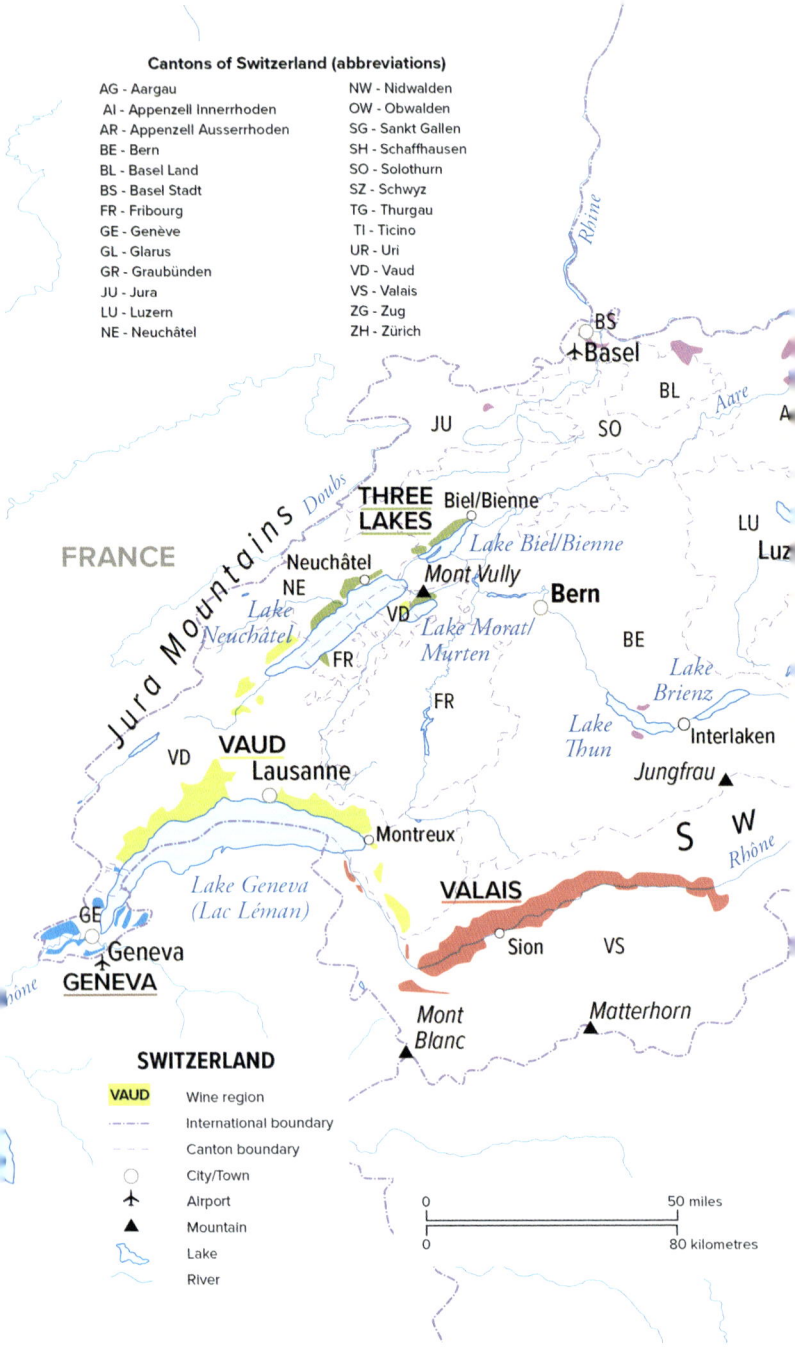

Cantons of Switzerland (abbreviations)

AG - Aargau
AI - Appenzell Innerrhoden
AR - Appenzell Ausserrhoden
BE - Bern
BL - Basel Land
BS - Basel Stadt
FR - Fribourg
GE - Genève
GL - Glarus
GR - Graubünden
JU - Jura
LU - Luzern
NE - Neuchâtel

NW - Nidwalden
OW - Obwalden
SG - Sankt Gallen
SH - Schaffhausen
SO - Solothurn
SZ - Schwyz
TG - Thurgau
TI - Ticino
UR - Uri
VD - Vaud
VS - Valais
ZG - Zug
ZH - Zürich

Basel
BS
BL
Aare
JU
SO
A

Rhine

THREE LAKES
Biel/Bienne
Lake Biel/Bienne
LU
Luz

FRANCE

Doubs

Neuchâtel
NE
Mont Vully
Bern
Lake
Neuchâtel
VD
Lake Morat/
Murten
BE
Lake
Brienz
FR
FR
Lake
Thun
Interlaken
Jura Mountains
VAUD
VD
Lausanne
Jungfraü
S   W
Rhône
Montreux
VALAIS
Lake Geneva
(Lac Léman)
VS
GE
Sion
Geneva
GENEVA
Rhône
Mont
Blanc
Matterhorn

SWITZERLAND

VAUD	Wine region
	International boundary
	Canton boundary
○	City/Town
✈	Airport
▲	Mountain
	Lake
	River

0	50 miles
0	80 kilometres

Danube

N

GERMANY

SH

Konstanz

Lake Constance

TG

Zürich

St Gallen

ZH

AR

GERMAN-SPEAKING
REGION

AI

Lake
Zürich

SG

LIECHTENSTEIN

AUSTRIA

ZG   Zug

▲Rigi

SZ

Vaduz

GL

NW

Lake
Luzern

Rhine

Chur

Inn

▲

Titlis

UR

A   l   p   s

GR

S

St Moritz

Piz Bernina   ▲

TI

TICINO

Lake
Maggiore

Lugano

Lake
Lugano

ITALY

Milan

Introduction

It may be small, but Switzerland's reputation is anything but. Towering snow-covered peaks, mirror-like lakes and storybook villages set the scene for world-class skiing, legendary hotels and a standard of living few can rival. Precision watches, efficient public transport and the ubiquitous Swiss Army knife add to the nation's reputation for quality and ingenuity. And then there's the food: welcome to the land of cheese and chocolate.

But there's one thing Switzerland is generally not known for – its wine. Swiss wine rarely makes it beyond the country's borders, not because it isn't worth sharing, but because there simply isn't enough to go around. Domestic production meets less than half the total demand for wine, so very little is exported.

Switzerland's size gives little indication of the complexity and diversity of its vineyards. For a start, there are over 250 grape varieties: local gems like Chasselas, Räuschling, Gamaret and Cornalin thrive alongside international favourites. Vineyards cling to mountain slopes; stone terraces, some centuries old, require constant upkeep. The next generation of Swiss winemakers, many of whom have trained abroad, are now taking the reins, bringing fresh perspectives while honouring their roots.

The Swiss take their natural surroundings seriously (hiking is a national pastime), living in harmony with the mountains, lakes and rivers that shape their way of life. The Swiss Alps, known as Europe's 'water tower', feed the continent's great rivers, while the vineyards – often family-owned for generations – are a key part of Switzerland's heritage.

The country's reputation for quality, innovation and hospitality is well-earned; Swiss hotels and restaurants offer an abundance of choice. And with its highly coordinated network of trains, buses, boats and motorways, travelling is as seamless as it is scenic. There's never been a better time to visit this extraordinary – and unsung – wine country.

Terraced vineyards, Valais

History

The history of wine in Switzerland goes back at least as far as Roman times. Wine amphorae originating from Italy and France, found in the northeast of the country, prove that the locals were drinking wines from abroad around the time of Caesar's conquest. There is every reason to believe that the Romans brought their wine-drinking habits with them and planted vines for local production.

'The Wine Festival' by Albert Anker, 1866

Rome, Charlemagne and the Church

In the Dark Ages, long before the idea of Switzerland was born, there is ample evidence of vineyards on Swiss territory, and the central role the church played in the cultivation of vines and the production of wine. The Abbey of St Maurice, founded 1,500 years ago in modern-day Valais, still has its own vineyard. In the 8th century, Bishop

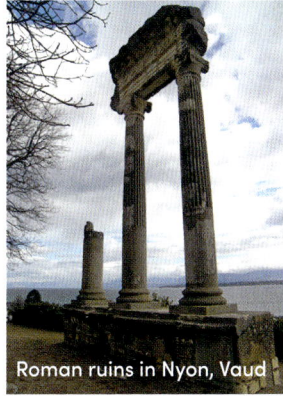
Roman ruins in Nyon, Vaud

Tello of the diocese of Chur in modern day Graubünden, bequeathed vineyards to nearby Disentis Abbey. The first Holy Roman Emperor, Charlemagne, owned vineyards in the year 814 near Orbe (they are commemorated today in the '814' wines of Château d'Eclépens). But it is the precipitous vineyards of Lavaux in Vaud (see p30) that tell the most compelling story. In the 11th century, Benedictine and Cistercian monks cleared forests, sculpted terraces and planted vineyards supported by miles of stone walls. In continuous production ever since, Lavaux was recognized by UNESCO as a World Heritage Site in 2007. Ancient Lavaux estates like Clos des Abbayes and Clos des Moines are now owned by the city of Lausanne, making it one of the largest wine producers in the canton of Vaud.

Historic castles with wine links are in every part of Switzerland. Schloss Salenegg in canton Graubünden, which was producing wines in 1068, is one of the oldest winemaking

Bust of Charlemagne

Schloss Salenegg, Graubünden

estates in Europe. Castello di Morcote in canton Ticino is a rare medieval fort with a Roman lookout tower set above the vineyards. Château d'Aigle in canton Vaud dates to the 12th century and is surrounded by vineyards that have been on the site even longer. Today it houses a wine museum which was designed specifically to safeguard the country's rich viticultural heritage (see p137). In Vaud and Valais there are over 30 historic and aristocratic winemaking estates. Many of these – like the 16th-century Château de Villa in Valais, the ruins of which have been transformed into a wine bar and restaurant (see p184) – are open to the public.

Château d'Aigle, Vaud

Ancient grapes

In the decades following the formation of the Old Swiss Confederacy in 1291, ancient native grape varieties like Humagne Blanche, Rèze and Completer (all still in production today) appear in written documents for the first time. The first Pinot Noir to be grown in Switzerland arrived in the 15th century, when Marie of Burgundy gave vines to the people of Morges and St Prex to thank them for giving her shelter while pregnant during the plague. Today, the Servagnin de Morges appellation is reserved for wines made from vines related to that original stock (the name Servagnin is an ancient synonym for Pinot Noir).

The Swiss enthusiastically celebrate their venerable wine history – and never more so than with Chasselas, the national grape, first mentioned in writing in 1654. It's the star of the Fête des Vignerons, held every 20-25 years in Vevey since 1797, when growers and producers pay homage to the grape in song and dance in a month-long festival that attracts thousands.

Thomas Cook and the rise of tourism

Tourism in Switzerland has a more recent but no less colourful history.

It began with Thomas Cook, who revolutionized travel when he organized the very first group trip to Switzerland in the summer of 1863 (the same year that the Red Cross was launched in Geneva). Seven people from the Junior United Alpine Club left England on a three-week journey, and visited the lakes and mountains of Switzerland by train, coach, steamship, mule and on foot. Little did they or Cook know

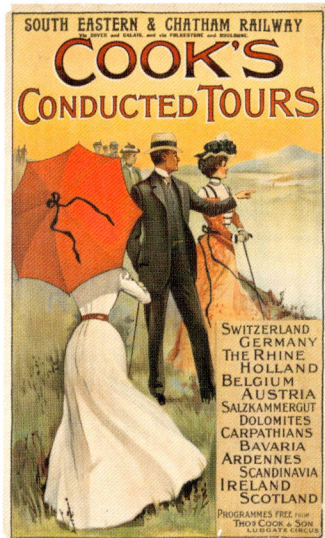

SOUTH EASTERN & CHATHAM RAILWAY
Via DOVER and CALAIS, and via FOLKESTONE and BOULOGNE.

COOK'S CONDUCTED TOURS

SWITZERLAND
GERMANY
THE RHINE
HOLLAND
BELGIUM
AUSTRIA
SALZKAMMERGUT
DOLOMITES
CARPATHIANS
BAVARIA
ARDENNES
SCANDINAVIA
IRELAND
SCOTLAND

PROGRAMMES FREE FROM
THOS COOK & SON
LUDGATE CIRCUS.

Jungfrau railway c.1912

the seismic significance of this trip. 'It was a journey that launched mass tourism. It was an invasion that created modern Switzerland,' the Swiss expert Diccon Bewes noted.

Switzerland was already part of the Grand Tour of Europe, a customary rite of passage for the wealthy, and for writers and artists. Lord Byron, JMW Turner, Charles Dickens and Wordsworth were all inspired by their visits. Thomas Cook's success came from opening up Switzerland to the Victorian middle classes: his genius was to take advantage of cheap travel enabled by the new railways.

At the time, Switzerland was recovering from its 1847 civil war (which resulted in the creation of the country as the federal state we know today); it was a relatively poor and largely rural country. This new generation of principally British tourists had to forgo modern conveniences, but hotels started to appear and over the next 50 years more railway lines were built, including rack railways linking Visp to Zermatt (over 1,600m/5,250ft) and Zermatt to Gornergrat (over 3,000m/9,843ft). The Jungfrau railway, which opened in 1912 and climbs to 3,500m (11,483ft), is still Europe's highest railway.

Phylloxera and the emergence of modern Swiss viticulture

While the Swiss invention of milk chocolate in 1875 and

the publication of the classic children's tale Heidi in 1880 (with 50 million sales one of the best-selling books of all time – see p44) added to the growing appeal of Switzerland, winemakers were distracted by the arrival of a virulent vine pest. Phylloxera, a louse which feeds on the roots of grapevines, arrived in Europe from the USA in the 1850s, and by the end of the century had devastated the vineyards of France. It was first recorded in Switzerland in 1871; over the following decades it wreaked havoc.

Viticulture faced many other pressures: the loss of labour to the textile and machinery industries, increasing competition from breweries and spirits producers and cheap foreign wine imported by the growing rail network – not to mention the temperance movement. When Thomas Cook's party first came to Switzerland, there were 30,000 hectares of vineyard in Switzerland (the size of Burgundy today); by the 1930s it had shrunk to just over one-third of that. And, by all accounts, the output was unremarkable – the wines tended to be dull, thin and neutral. Numerous vineyards were replanted with international grape varieties like Pinot Noir, Gamay, Merlot and Syrah in place of the old native varieties.

Swiss wine being shipped in Bulle, Fribourg c. 1920

Swiss wine in the 21st century

In the 1950s the government set recommended prices and restricted imports in an effort to protect Swiss wine, but the focus on quantity over quality led to massive surpluses of white wine (which was most of Swiss production). Then, as Switzerland regulated its trade with the European Union, the measures were relaxed; today the vineyard area has recovered to about half its historical size at around 15,000 hectares. Producers now started to prioritize quality over quantity. In 1988 Geneva was the first canton to establish an AOC (Appellation d'Origine Contrôlée) for its wines. The other cantons of Switzerland followed soon after.

In the 21st century a new generation of leading producers, many of whom served their apprenticeships in the wine regions of wider Europe and beyond, have brought back skills and experiences that help them deliver vastly better wines. They also see the value of continuing to revive Switzerland's indigenous grape varieties, some of which had almost disappeared. This is a smart way not only of

Vineyards overlooking Sion, Valais

differentiating their local wines from wine imports but also of preserving the country's viticultural heritage of old varieties and old vines.

Looking ahead, Switzerland is well-positioned to claim a more prominent place on the global wine stage. Growing international interest as far afield as the USA and Asia, smarter strategies to increase exports and renewed pride in native grape varieties promise an exciting new chapter. Seasoned Swiss producers – deeply rooted in tradition yet open to innovation – are rising to meet the challenges of climate change. The country's complex mosaic of Alpine climates and terroirs offers a unique canvas for experimentation, with winemakers embracing new disease-resistant grapes and more sustainable vineyard practices, including a shift towards organic and biodynamic production. At the same time, the emergence of wine tourism is a huge opportunity: more vineyard trails, winery tours, wine experiences and events will further enhance the country's appeal as a travel destination and help to connect Swiss wines with a broader global audience.

Geography

Switzerland is small – a third the size of England – but its geography is rich and varied. Within this compact area, its 15,000 hectares of vineyards place it (surprisingly) among the top 20 wine-producing countries in the world.

The Dents du Midi behind Château de Chillon on Lake Geneva

Sopraceneri, Ticino

Wine is produced in every one of the country's 26 cantons, which are divided into six wine regions. Four are in the west: Valais, Vaud, Geneva and Three Lakes; collectively known as Suisse Romande, they cover around three-quarters of the entire vineyard area. The German-speaking cantons in the north, centre and east of the country represent around one-fifth of the vineyards. Ticino, the Italian-speaking canton in the south, makes up just under a tenth of the total wine-growing area.

Switzerland's mountains provide some of the most memorable vistas and breathtaking backdrops anywhere in the world of wine. The Alps and the Jura mountains, which together cover nearly three-quarters of the entire country, were created over the course of several million years as the African and Eurasian tectonic plates smashed into one another, causing the land to buckle upwards.

'Within this dramatic landscape, Switzerland boasts some of the highest vineyards in Europe'

Within this dramatic landscape, Switzerland boasts some of the highest vineyards in Europe. In Valais they rise to some 1,100m (3,600ft) – the same average height as the vineyards in the foothills of the Andes, in Argentina's Mendoza region. Switzerland's latitude between the 45th and the 47th parallels makes it suitable for wine production, but much of the land is too high, with terrain that renders viticulture impossible, so vines are planted only in the most favourable sites. The ecosystem of glaciers, mountains, rivers and lakes creates favourable grape-growing conditions.

The Alps dominate the land. More than half of the range's giant peaks, which reach heights of 4,000m (13,100ft) or more, are on Swiss territory. Their formation is directly linked to another major feature of the Swiss landscape: its 1,800 glaciers, the remains of the thick layer of ice that covered the country in the last Ice Age. The Aletsch Glacier in canton Valais is the biggest in the Alps and the larger Jungfrau-Aletsch area was declared a UNESCO World Heritage site in 2001. Since the Ice Age ended around 15,000 years ago, the glaciers have been retreating, laying down deposits carried along by the melting ice. These so-called moraines – a mixture of rock, boulders and gravel – are a defining component of the soils in every Swiss wine region, although they are just one of many elements found in the ground.

The mountain snowmelt and glaciers feed the country's many rivers and lakes, making Switzerland the water tower of Europe. All the Continent's principal waterways can trace their source to the Alps: canton Graubünden in the east is the source of the Rhine as well as the Inn, a tributary of the

Riederalp near Aletsch, with the Matterhorn rising centre stage

Danube; high up in canton Valais in the south-west, the meltwater from the Rhône Glacier feeds the river of the same name. In fact, the source springs of the Rhône and the Rhine are just 22 km (14 miles) apart. On the south side of the Alps the river

Aletsch Glacier

Ticino, which gives its name to the canton, flows into the Po. Switzerland might reasonably claim to be the key that unlocks many of the great wine regions of Europe, since without these rivers the vineyards of France, Germany, Italy and Austria may never have existed.

The rivers feed Switzerland's countless lakes, many of which are framed by vineyards. Some of the biggest are shared with neighbouring countries: Lake Geneva with France, Lake Constance with Germany and Austria and Lakes Maggiore and Lugano with Italy. Lakes Neuchâtel,

View across Lake Geneva from the vineyards of Lavaux, Vaud

Lucerne and Zürich are the large lakes entirely within Switzerland. The frequent boat services that connect the towns and villages on these and smaller lakes offer one of the more relaxing ways to soak up the landscape and take in panoramic views of the vineyards and their surroundings.

The country's unique topography of sloping lake shores, riverbanks and steep-sided valleys allows vines to be planted on sites which can maximize their exposure to the sun. The mountains protect the vineyards from cold winds and harsh weather, while the numerous bodies of water moderate the climate and create favourable conditions for vines. The majority of the vineyards are planted on south-facing slopes, but some point east, west and even north depending on the grape variety and local climate.

Despite its size, Switzerland's Alpine terrain creates a diversity of local climates and a range of different growing conditions. The largely continental climate is moderated by the rivers and lakes, while the *föhn* (a warm, dry, downslope mountain wind) helps the grapes to ripen fully. The north

side of the Alps enjoys plenty of sunshine, but rainfall can be low so the vineyards require irrigation with mountain water. Further north, there is significantly less sunshine, and average temperatures are the lowest of all the wine regions. By contrast on the south side of the Alps, Mediterranean conditions prevail. It is sunnier here than in the north, but there is also more than three times the rainfall. This rain is often heavy, and strong hailstorms are not unusual. Climate change is leading to warmer conditions that may benefit Swiss wine producers, but is also creating challenges as the ready availability of water from the mountains comes increasingly under threat.

There is an equal diversity of soils in the vineyards. The Alps, the Jura and the plain in between form three distinct geological zones. This soil diversity is part of the reason for the large number of grape varieties growing here – some familiar, but many unique to Switzerland. (See **Wine Regions of Switzerland** p26 and **Wine styles and grape varieties** p52.)

The source of the Rhône at the foot of the Rhône Glacier in Oberwald, Valais

Wine regions of Switzerland

From vertiginous terraces that cling perilously to the mountainside to broad sweeps of lakeside vines that stretch into the sunset, the wine regions of Switzerland are as varied as they are spectacularly beautiful.

Chamoson, Valais

Switzerland and its 2,500 wine producers are divided into six regions. Four of these – **Valais, Vaud, Geneva** and **Ticino** – are defined by a single canton. **Deutschschweiz** (**the German-speaking Region**) covers 16 cantons, and **Three Lakes** covers the cantons of Neuchâtel, Bern, Fribourg and overlaps with a small part of Vaud.

Domestic demand is high, so very little wine is exported. This leads to a degree of rivalry between the different regions, which spend as much time and effort competing with each other as they do with foreign wine imports.

For details on each grape variety below, see **Wine styles and grape varieties** (p52).

Valais

One in every three bottles of wine produced in Switzerland comes from Valais. The largest and most mountainous wine region, its steep, U-shaped valley was carved by the retreating Rhône Glacier 20,000 years ago. The Rhône is more commonly associated with France, but its actual source is high up in the east of Valais. From there it cascades into the valley, increasing in volume and speed as it flows past the vineyard slopes and empties into Lake Geneva.

Twenty peaks over 4,000m (13,123ft), including the famous Matterhorn, give this region a distinctly Alpine look and feel. Valais is protected by the Alps to the south, and the warming *föhn* wind and dry, sunny climate provide ideal growing conditions. Valais has the lowest rainfall in Switzerland, so the vines are irrigated with water from the Alpine snowmelt and glacial runoff. A network

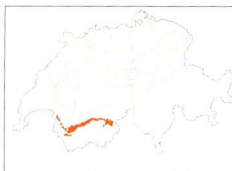

The Matterhorn, Valais

A traditional *bisse* and hiking trail, Valais

of man-made irrigation channels, called *bisses*, follow the contours of the slopes and side valleys; the oldest date back to at least the 13th century. Some are still used in agriculture today, while others have become hiking trails.

About a third of the grapes grown here are indigenous. The country's ubiquitous white wine grape, the native Chasselas (known as Fendant in Valais), is seeing competition from other native white varieties such as Petite Arvine. Other notable native grapes include Humagne Blanche and Amigne. Some other white grapes may be familiar, but not their local names: Malvoisie for Pinot Gris, Ermitage for Marsanne, Johannisberg for Silvaner and Heida or Païen for Savagnin Blanc.

Red wine varieties account for almost 60% of the region's vineyards, where local reds like Cornalin and Humagne Rouge grow alongside Pinot Noir and Gamay – the latter two commonly making up the easy-drinking Dôle blend. Syrah also grows well, as it should: this is the Rhône Valley after all.

In Valais, several of the white varieties also produce medium-sweet wines labelled *mi-flétri* and sweet *flétri* wines. Look out for wines bearing the Grain Noble ConfidenCiel neck label, which guarantees their quality.

Vin des glaciers is a local speciality made high up in Val d'Anniviers near Sierre. This dry oxidative wine, aged in larch casks, was traditionally made with Rèze (see p58), but these days is primarily a Marsanne-based blend. It's sometimes known as the 'sherry of the Alps': as the level in the casks goes down, they are topped up with new vintages – a version of the solera system used to make sherry.

Evidence of the rich geological history of this most Alpine of regions is found in the varied soils. Granite prevails in Lower Valais, between Martigny and Saillon in the west of the region, and loess and limestone appear in some places. Heading further east to Sion and Sierre, the soils are characterized by moraines (glacial deposits) and either chalk or schist (resembling slate). At the higher, eastern end of the region in Upper Valais, limestone defines the soils.

Many of the vines are planted on slopes that can be vertiginously steep – as much as 90% in places – and dry-stone walls run across the hillsides. Since the stones are not held together by cement, the gaps in between offer a safe refuge to lizards, butterflies and other wildlife.

The warm climate allows some of the vineyards to be planted at altitudes over 750m (2,460ft): in Visperterminen in the east of Valais they climb to 1,150m (3,773ft) – among the highest in Europe. The phylloxera pest, which destroyed most of Europe's vineyards at the end of the 19th century, couldn't survive at such altitudes, and thousands of ungrafted (pre-phylloxera) Savagnin Blanc vines survive to this day.

Dotted around the landscape are small huts, called *guérites*, where the growers stored tools and equipment. Some date back centuries and are still in use; others are being repurposed as rustic picnic spots – with glorious views – in the middle of the vineyards.

Valais is also home to

Visperterminen, Valais

Switzerland's largest single producer – the former cooperative Provins (see p122), which makes about six percent of all Swiss wine. Based in Sion, Provins was formed almost a century ago

Lower Valais

when small producers, some with just a few rows of vines passed down from one generation to the next, were struggling to cope with over-production, foreign wine imports and economic crisis. Provins now has 20 different ranges made from the grapes of around 1,000 growers; it also has six Provins shops and a wine bar in Sion.

Vaud

The crescent-shaped Lake Geneva, known locally as Lac Léman, is one of the largest lakes in western Europe. This impressive body of water helps to regulate temperature

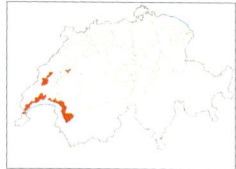

and ensures favourable conditions for growing grapes. On the northern shore, the vineyards of Vaud dominate the landscape and account for one quarter of Switzerland's wine production, making Vaud the second biggest wine region.

Vaud is the only region of Switzerland where more white wine is produced than red, although the latter is increasing. It encompasses six distinct subregions – three alongside the lake and three inland to the north, each with its own AOC. Yet for all the variations in the vineyards of Vaud, there is one common feature: Chasselas, the most widely planted Swiss white grape, originated here and accounts for over 60% of the Vaud vineyards. Chardonnay and Pinot Gris are also planted, and a locally developed white variety called

Doral (see p64), created from Chasselas and Chardonnay, is worth trying. The major red wine varieties are Pinot Noir and Gamay, sold both as a popular blend called Salvagnin and as single varietals. Next come two specially developed Swiss varieties, Gamaret and Garanoir (see p65), which are becoming increasingly popular.

La Côte

The westernmost area, between Geneva and Lausanne, represents just over half of the Vaud vineyards. The gentle vineyard slopes here are protected from the cold north winds by the Jura mountains. The villages of Mont-sur-Rolle and Féchy are home to some of the more notable wines.

Lavaux

Further east, between Lausanne and Montreux, the steep slopes of Lavaux look down on the widest and deepest section of Lake Geneva. These terraced vineyards follow the contours of the land for almost 30km (20 miles) virtually without interruption. Built in the 11th century when Benedictine and Cistercian monasteries controlled the area, and in continuous use ever since, the Lavaux vineyards were designated a World Heritage site by UNESCO in 2007. Erosion of the soil is a constant challenge, however; the winemakers are also stonemasons, keeping the 450km (280 miles) of old walls maintained.

The heritage of this striking region is taken very seriously, right down to the small cabins called *capites*, which in the past were used for storing tools; many of them are listed monuments.

Lavaux is called 'the land of the three suns' for good reason. The vines benefit from the direct sunlight, the sun's reflection off the lake and the heat of the sun absorbed by the walled terraces, which keep warming the vines long after the sun has set. There is even a fourth 'sun' that turns the lake into a thermal reservoir, tempering the local climate.

If Lavaux is the jewel in the crown of the vineyards of Vaud (if not all of Switzerland), then the most precious

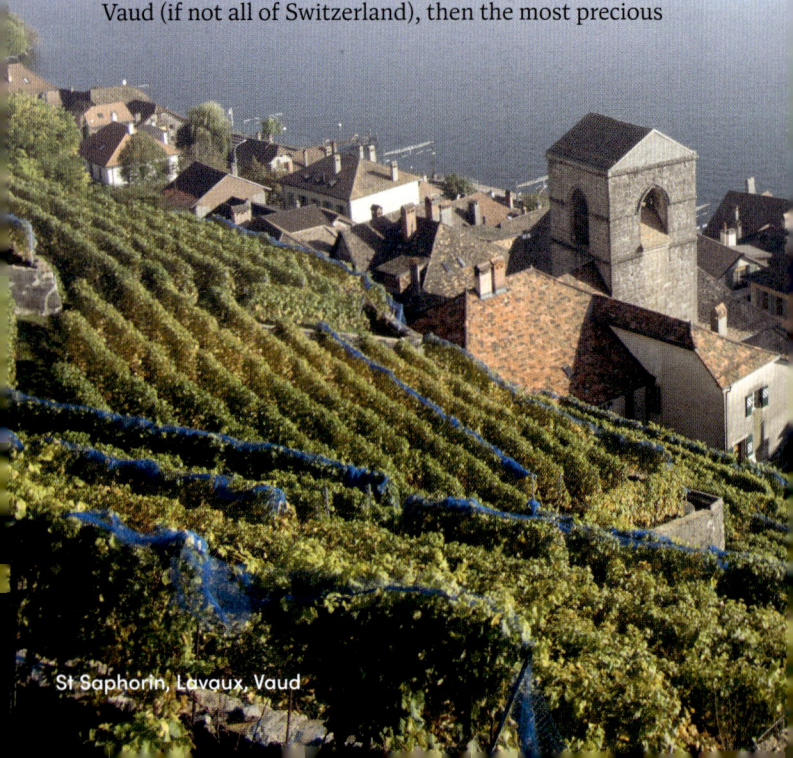

St Saphorin, Lavaux, Vaud

gems are its Grand Cru sites:
Dézaley and Calamin, each
with its own AOC. The clay
and limestone soil in these
small 'crus' near the village of
Epesses lie on puddingstone
beds, which produce wines

Féchy, La Côte

with notable weight and character, capable of long ageing,
that are revered by locals and connoisseurs alike.

Chablais

At the eastern end of Lake Geneva, Chablais runs from
Villeneuve to Bex and is overlooked by the imposing Dents
du Midi mountain range. In these Alpine foothills, the soils
are a mix of rock and limestone. The presence of boulders
in the vineyards is a clear sign of the Alpine influence on
Chablais, as is the historical evidence. In 1584 a major
earthquake caused a massive landslide that covered the
village of Yvorne, whose wines reveal a marked mineral
character. The proximity of Chablais to Valais means that it

Autumn panorama, Chablais

also benefits from the warming *föhn* wind, helping to create richer, more powerful wines.

Bonvillars

North of Lausanne, Bonvillars wraps around the medieval town of Grandson at the southern end of Lake Neuchâtel. It produces mainly Chasselas whites, Pinot Noir reds and rosé wines called *Oeil de Perdrix* (the name used in nearby Three Lakes). Soils of limestone rock and gravel impart characteristic minerality to the local wines. Some of the vineyard sites are marked by menhirs, recalling a prehistoric age. Oddly, the village of Champagne labels some of its wines 'C-ampagne', since the Champagne appellation in France successfully challenged its right to use its own village name.

Truffle market, Bonvillars

Côtes de l'Orbe

This is an even smaller area, located south of Lake Neuchâtel. The town of Orbe was a staging post between Pontarlier (in France) and Lausanne on the Via Francigena – the ancient pilgrimage route from Canterbury to Rome. Centuries-

old documents record the emperor Charlemagne owning vineyards nearby in the year 814. Three-quarters of the vineyards produce red wines primarily from Gamay, Pinot Noir, Gamaret and Garanoir. The main white varieties are Chasselas, Doral and Pinot Gris.

Vully

The smallest of the subregions is a unique wine-growing area in Switzerland, since it straddles two cantons: Vaud and Freiburg (Fribourg). It sits on the line of a figurative ditch called the *Röstigraben* (named after the popular Bernese *rösti*

Springtime, Côtes de l'Orbe

Lake Morat, Vully

potato dish), with German language, culture and cuisine on one side, French on the other. The vineyards are squeezed between Lakes Neuchâtel and Morat (or Murtensee), planted on Jurassic clay and limestone soil. Chasselas and Pinot Noir are the principal white and red varieties, but local specialities such as Gewürztraminer and Freisamer whites and Merlot and Gamaret reds are also produced.

In this multifaceted agglomeration of vineyards all roads lead to Lausanne: cantonal capital, Olympic capital and the capital of Swiss gastronomy, with 11 Michelin-starred restaurants (including the three-star Restaurant de l'Hôtel de Ville at Crissier) and over 100 GaultMillau restaurants. (See also Fête des Vignerons, p15.)

Geneva

Geneva is one of the smallest cantons but the fourth-largest and most densely planted wine region, accounting for a tenth of all Swiss vineyards. There are many influences on the vines: the Jura mountains and the pre-Alps, the lake itself and the river Rhône. In most cases, the vineyards are on gentle slopes – this is the region with the smallest difference between highest and lowest points. Geneva was the first Swiss canton to launch an AOC, in 1988, and has since added a further 22 AOC Premier Cru appellations. The producers here also like to experiment, which probably explains why so many grape varieties are authorized for production: 24 white and 21 red.

In the late 1990s, reds used to outnumber whites, but now account for well over half of production. While Gamay dominates, it is steadily being replaced by Pinot Noir, Gamaret, Merlot and Garanoir. Chasselas (sometimes called Perlan – see p55) is the most important white grape, but is making way for other non-native varieties such as Chardonnay, Sauvignon Blanc, Aligoté and Viognier. Most of the wineries also produce sparkling wines.

Stormy skies over the Mandement, Geneva

Rive Droite

To the west is the Right Bank of the river Rhône, the largest of the three subregions, which accounts for two-thirds of Geneva production. Rive Droite also encompasses the Mandement, ancient land that used to belong to the Bishop of Geneva. The area includes Satigny, the single biggest wine-growing commune in all Switzerland, and the pretty nearby village of Dardagny, known for fine Pinot Noir. The soil is largely sandstone, shale and marl. Around a third of Geneva's wines are produced by the cooperative Cave de Genève, based in Satigny.

Entre Arve et Rhône

The area between Arve and Rhône runs south of the river Rhône to the border with France. Glacial deposits from the surrounding mountains make the soil rich in limestone and gravel, resulting in wines with finesse and elegance.

Entre Arve et Lac, Geneva

Entre Arve et Lac

To the east is the smallest subregion, between Arve and Lake, which follows the Lake Geneva shoreline from Cologny to Hermance. The protective influence of the neighbouring French Alps and the moraine-rich soil ensure well-ripened grapes and aromatic wines.

Just under 10% of Geneva's vineyards are located on

Lake Neuchâtel

French territory in two small free-zone areas whose origins are rooted in 200 years of topsy-turvy history. These wines can be classified as AOC Geneva.

Three Lakes

Pinot Noir is ubiquitous in this, the smallest wine region in Switzerland where it is made into red, rosé and sparkling wines. *Oeil de Perdrix* ('partridge's eye') is the name given to its rosés, though in spite of efforts to protect it the term has since spread to other regions.

The Three Lakes region comprises two languages (Trois Lacs/Drei Seen), three lakes – Neuchâtel, Biel/Bienne and Morat/Murten – and four cantons, accounting for seven percent of the country's vineyards. The invisible line called

the *Röstigraben* that divides it is explained in the section on Vully (see p35).

The biggest area (AOC Neuchâtel) runs along the western side of Lake Neuchâtel, accounting for almost two-thirds of the region. The fairly dry, sunny

Auvernier, Lake Neuchâtel

climate is moderated by the lake, which makes the winters less harsh, while the Jura mountains provide protection from cold north winds and rain from the west. Limestone is the overriding characteristic of the soil (much as it is in nearby Burgundy), which is why Pinot Noir thrives here.

Oeil de Perdrix (below) is made using the *saignée* method of light contact with the skins and is best drunk young, before the fruit flavours fade. Pinot Noir is also vinified as a white wine called *Perdrix Blanche*. The region has a long tradition of producing *méthode traditionnelle* sparkling wine using Pinot Noir.

Cressier, Auvernier and Cortaillod are important winemaking villages along the shores of the lake, the latter bestowing its name on a local variant of Pinot Noir. More than half of the white wines are made with Chasselas, which includes an unfiltered speciality called *Non-Filtré* (see p77).

White varieties are more important in canton Bern (AOC Bielersee), which represents just under a quarter of the region, and in Fribourg (Freiburg) with its two small AOCs (Vully and Cheyres). Vully on the north shore of Lake Morat (Murtensee) shares its appellation with neighbouring Vaud; Cheyres is on the south shore of Lake Neuchâtel. Chasselas dominates, while other whites include Chardonnay and Pinot Gris. Sauvignon Blanc is present in Vully and Freisamer (a mix of Silvaner and Pinot Gris) in Cheyres.

German-speaking Region

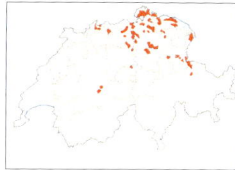

Also known as *Deutschschweiz*, this region represents 16 of Switzerland's 26 cantons and covers about a fifth of its vineyards. The six most important cantons are **Zürich, Schaffhausen, Graubünden, Aargau, Thurgau** and **Sankt Gallen**. The many lakes and rivers in this vast plateau region exert a strong influence on the vines by helping to regulate the climate, as does the warming *föhn* wind.

Wine is not the principal activity for the vast majority of growers. Only about one in ten are large enough estates to convert their grape harvest to wine. The rest sell their grapes to the bigger producers, while keeping their small vineyard plots in the family as their fathers did before them and their fathers' fathers before that.

Pinot Noir, which accounts for over 50% of the vines here, is often called Blauburgunder, meaning 'the blue grape from Burgundy'. Among the white grapes, Riesling-Silvaner (otherwise known as Müller-Thurgau – see p64) is widely planted. Elsewhere, notable native varieties such as Räuschling and Completer play an important role alongside Chardonnay, Pinot Gris (commonly called Grauburgunder) and Sauvignon Blanc.

Zürich

The vineyards of Zürich form the largest single area in the region, though they were 10 times bigger at the end of the

Stäfa, Zürich

Schloss Laufen, Rhine Falls, Schaffhausen

19th century: the combined effects of urban and industrial expansion, which created Switzerland's largest city, and the devastation wreaked in the vineyards by phylloxera led to a significant decline in wine production. Pinot Noir accounts for over two-fifths of the region and Müller-Thurgau another fifth. Sauvignon Blanc, Chardonnay and Pinot Gris are important white varieties, as is the local speciality Räuschling. Winegrower cooperatives represent about half of production.

Schaffhausen

At the northern tip of Switzerland, canton Schaffhausen is known for the Rhine Falls – the most powerful waterfall in Europe. In the vineyards, almost 60% are planted with Pinot Noir, which thrives in the mild, dry climate and chalky soils. Müller-Thurgau is the leading white grape; other varieties include Chardonnay, Sauvignon Blanc and Pinot Gris. Winegrower cooperatives represent around 85% of production here.

Graubünden

The most significant vineyard area is the Bündner Herrschaft, a small pocket near the ancient bishopric of

Chur and close to Liechtenstein. Flanked by the Alps on all sides, the vineyards are barely 100km (60 miles) from the two sources of the river Rhine, which flows past the villages of Malans, Jenins and Fläsch. The mountains to the north protect the vines from cold winds and help to create a mild continental climate, making this the region's warmest area.

The soils are rich in limestone and clay, with slate and loess deposits. These are the result of the retreating ice masses from the Rhine Valley 15,000 years ago as well as the constant movement of the surrounding mountains. The big difference in temperature between daytime and night-time gives a real freshness to the wines, while the warming *föhn* wind helps ripen the grapes.

Despite the area's centuries-old wine tradition, its fame for top-quality wines is relatively recent. Viticulture took over from polyculture in the 1970s when important changes took place in both the vineyards and cellars, such as riper harvests, new varieties and oak ageing. Pinot Noir flourishes here and accounts for over 70% of plantings; the wines deliver the delicate aromas and haunting sensuality that are true to this variety's elegance and finesse at its best. Chardonnay and Pinot Blanc are the main white

Alter Torkel – Huus vum Bündner Wii restaurant, Graubünden (see p140)

grapes along with Completer, a local speciality and one of the country's oldest varieties. First documented in 1321, it is considered a rarity even in Switzerland but is well worth seeking out.

The village of Maienfeld was the setting for the famous children's story Heidi, possibly the best-known Swiss novel of all time and one of the world's best-selling books. Heidi is celebrated throughout the area, which the local tourist board has branded 'Heidiland', and includes Heididorf – a recreated period village open to visitors.

Aargau

To the north-west of Zürich, Aargau is home to the Habsburg castle, which gave the dynasty its name. One thousand years ago the family held sway here before shifting its focus towards Austria. Many bodies of water flow through the canton, including the river Aare from which it takes its name, and these help to sustain a mild climate. The soils are generally rich in limestone that imparts a mineral character to the wines, half of which are Pinot Noir. The most widespread white variety is Müller-Thurgau, while Sauvignon Blanc and Chardonnay are also important.

Sunrise, Aargau

Thurgau

This relatively small wine-growing area, to the north-east of Zürich, is also known as an apple-producing region. The river Thur, a tributary of the Rhine, and Lake Constance to the north

Sunset, Thurgau

Fläsch, Graubünden

create a mild climate. The soils vary from sand and loam to limestone and moraine. Pinot Noir represents some 45% of the vines. The wines range in profile from simple and fruity to oak-aged and well-structured. Müller-Thurgau is the leading white variety in about one-fifth of the vineyards. Common white grapes are Pinot Gris and Sauvignon Blanc. The area is centred on Weinfelden and nearby Ottoberg.

Sankt Gallen

Between Zürich and Austria, Sankt Gallen is one of the smaller wine areas of the German-speaking Region. Most

Sankt Gallen

of the steep, south-facing vineyard slopes are on the west bank of the Rhine as it flows north into Lake Constance. Pinot Noir accounts for over half the vineyards and the principal white grapes are Müller-Thurgau, Chardonnay and Sauvignon Blanc.

Ticino

The Ticino region represents about eight percent of Switzerland's vineyards. A striking feature is how the old and the new sit side by side. In the north, the ancient method of training vines on pergolas of stone and wood is still used; grapes hang in the shade while cereals or vegetables grow on the ground below, though this is no longer common practice. In the south, numerous wineries have been rebuilt or expanded and have become leading examples of contemporary architecture, including work in Lugano by the well-known local architect Mario Botta.

Ticino could not be more different from the rest of Switzerland. The language is Italian, and the sub-Alpine, Mediterranean climate means more sunshine. It rains for a few days, mainly in spring, and when it does it pours: hailstorms are not unusual. Two large lakes – Maggiore and Lugano – stretch into neighbouring Italy and play a role in moderating the temperature.

Above all, a single variety has come to dominate in the

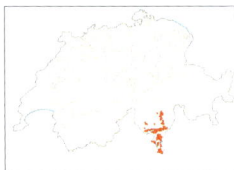

Terraced vineyards, Ticino

past 100 years: Merlot. Since World War II it has become the most planted variety here. Local *nostrano* red varieties like Bondola and Freisa used to define the wines of this region, but were supplanted by Merlot after phylloxera.

Ticino produces Merlot in a range of styles from fairly light to rich, full-bodied, carefully oaked wines that can hold their own against top Merlots from elsewhere. One of Ticino's big surprises is white Merlot (*Merlot Bianco*): some 25% of the variety's annual harvest is vinified this way, by avoiding contact with the dark grape skins. The absence of local white varieties was the catalyst for this innovation, though plantings of Chardonnay and Sauvignon Blanc are now increasing. Both unoaked and oaked versions of white Merlot are proving incredibly popular. Overall, it is estimated that white wines represent one-third of production; apart from a small amount of rosé, the balance is red.

Ticino consists of two subregions: Sopraceneri in the north and Sottoceneri to the south.

Sopraceneri has small vineyard plots on steep, fragmented terraces. The soils are rocky, with sand and silt, which results in austere wines that are designed for longer ageing. Near Ascona are the lowest vineyards in Switzerland – 200m (650ft) above sea level.

Sottoceneri vineyards are larger and situated on gentler slopes that are easier to work. The terroir of clay, limestone and volcanic rock, together with the warmer climate, create softer and more elegant wines.

In neighbouring Graubünden, a small enclave of vineyards produces wines in the Italian-speaking Val Mesolcina. The wines are vinified in Ticino and can be labelled either AOC Grigioni Mesolcina or AOC Ticino.

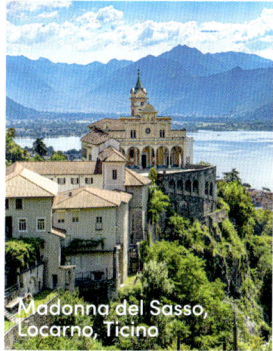
Madonna del Sasso, Locarno, Ticino

Swiss wine classifications and what they mean

Each canton sets its own rules for classifying wines. Regulated appellations started to appear less than 50 years ago and are not deeply embedded in the country's wine tradition. Since so many different grape varieties have been planted over the centuries, the rules permit a wide range to be grown. Watch out for terms such as 'Grand Cru', as they don't always mean the same as in other countries.

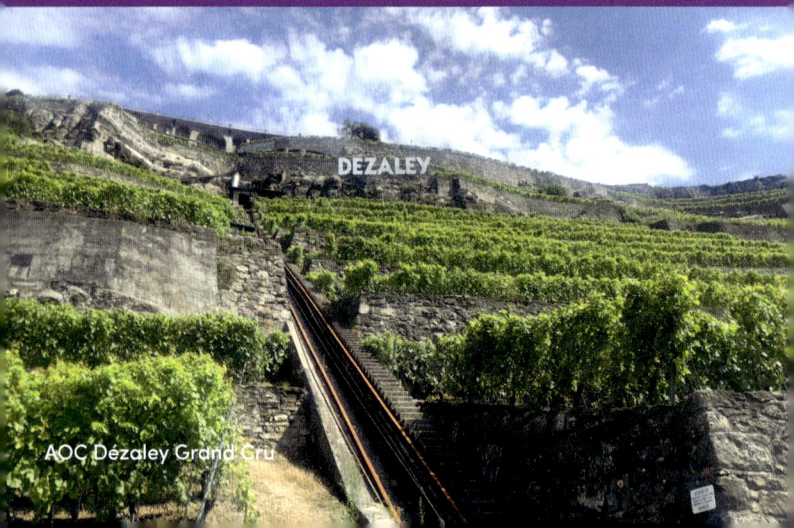

AOC Dézaley Grand Cru

Every one of the 26 Swiss cantons produces wine, from Valais to Vaud, and Thurgau to Ticino, though some, like Solothurn or Zug, make only very small quantities. Each individual canton sets its own laws covering wine production and labelling – a good illustration of what local sovereignty looks like in Switzerland. The Swiss approach means that the two regions straddling several cantons – Three Lakes and the German-speaking Region – do not have an AOC named after the region.

The appellation rules were only brought in for the first time in the late 1980s, so most of the 63 different names don't really resonate with wine drinkers and are often relegated to a label on the back of the bottle.

Cantonal appellations

The good news is that every canton (except for Fribourg) has a simple AOC or DOC bearing just the name of the canton, for instance:

AOC Valais covers the largest wine region of Switzerland and allows 31 white and 22 red grape varieties that must be shown on the label.

AOC Vaud designates the second biggest region, and allows 30 white and 31 red grape varieties. Wines made from the leading grape Chasselas make the place name prominent on the label, as the local terroir is considered an important factor.

Ticino DOC has colour-specific denominations – for example, Rosso del Ticino DOC for reds, Bianco del Ticino DOC for whites.

Regional appellations

These apply primarily in Vaud to designate different subregions such as AOC La Côte, AOC Lavaux and AOC Chablais, and in a few other cantons. In Vaud there are two Grand Cru appellations reserved for wines coming from the very best vineyard sites in the Lavaux subregion: Dézaley

AOC Graubünden

Grand Cru AOC and Calamin Grand Cru AOC.

Local appellations

Geneva is the only canton that also uses local appellations, of which there are 22, such as AOC Premier Cru Coteaux de Dardagny and AOC Premier Cru Coteau de Lully.

Other classifications

Grand Cru does not necessarily equate to premium quality as it does in many regions of neighbouring France. This classification, which is not an AOC, is regulated at a local level and is not used everywhere; in most cases, it takes the name of the commune or village. At least 90% of grapes like Chasselas or Pinot Noir must be grown in the named Grand Cru area, with the other 10% coming from the same region. The grape harvest must also achieve higher levels of ripeness, and the wines must pass a tasting panel each year to qualify.

In Valais, there are several communes – such as Sion, Chamoson or Vétroz – where producers seek the Grand Cru label for their best wines. Those made from native or traditional grapes (which vary by commune) and grown in the best vineyards are labelled with the name of the commune together with 'Grand Cru'.

Premier Grand Cru exists only in Vaud and has even stricter requirements. It currently covers 28 wines made from Chasselas, Pinot Noir, Gamay, Merlot, Gamaret and Garanoir. These wines are subjected to a rigorous annual tasting and must demonstrate the potential to age for at least 10 years.

Vin de Pays (VdP) and **Vin de Table** are used for wines that don't meet the requirements of the AOC regime. VdP wine (Landwein/IGT or *Indicazione Geografica Tipica*) can be labelled either VdP Suisse or, if the grapes come from an area covering more than one canton, VdP plus the name of the area – for example, VdP Romand (the French-speaking cantons). VdP wines made from the widely planted grapes Chasselas, Pinot Noir and Gamay may be given a broad geographic name linked to the variety such as Chasselas Romand or Pinot Noir Suisse. The price of a VdP wine will give you a good idea of its quality level, so don't be surprised to find some premium wines classified as VdP. Vin de Table (Tafelwein/Vino da Tavola) is the most basic classification for wine, according to the lowest permitted level of ripeness, so the quality and price are correspondingly low.

While restaurant wine lists tend not to mention the AOC/DOC, you can expect details of the canton, subregion and/or village for each producer. Wine retailers will often highlight the Grand Cru designation – and in the case of Dézaley and Calamin wines, the AOC is mentioned without fail as these two Grand Cru sites are universally recognized for their premium quality. Their reputation is akin to a brand name.

Wine styles and grape varieties

There are more than 250 grape varieties in Switzerland, many of them found nowhere else in the world, and the wines come in every conceivable style – red, white and rosé, dry, sweet and sparkling.

Merlot harvest at Vinattieri, Ligornetto, Ticino

Wine styles

Swiss wines have an Alpine freshness and precision. In much of the country, especially at higher altitudes, the summer growing season is characterized by long, sunny days and cool nights. This diurnal shift in temperature, much prized by winemakers, allows grapes to ripen fully while achieving good levels of acidity and keeping alcohol levels in check.

The wines come in every conceivable style in terms of colour, dryness, sweetness and effervescence. This is hardly a surprise given the significant differences in climate and terroir between the regions, not to mention the numerous grape varieties. Another reason for this diversity is that, historically, the Swiss were largely self-sufficient in wine. Until recently, strict limits on imported wines meant that Swiss wine producers were fulfilling almost the entire needs and diverse taste preferences of the country by themselves.

Switzerland produces equal amounts of white and red wines (and small amounts of rosé and sparkling). The long-term trend shows a gradual rise in red wine production, with white wine in slight decline.

It's very common to find single-varietal wines in Switzerland and, in most cases, the variety is clearly named on the front label. One exception is Vaud, where the indigenous Chasselas variety is often omitted from the label in favour of the village name, as the local terroir is considered the biggest influence on the wine's profile. Blended wines are usually given imaginative names that reveal little about the grape varieties.

Grape varieties

Switzerland, despite its modest vineyard area, is home to over 250 grape varieties. Three red varieties – Pinot Noir, Merlot and Gamay – dominate, covering over 40% of the vineyards. The most significant white grape is the indigenous Chasselas, which accounts for a quarter of the vineyard area. It is by far the country's leading white variety

Chasselas grapes, Domaine Blaise Duboux

and has great cultural significance. The remaining third consists of around 100 other noteworthy varieties, many of which are unique to Switzerland.

Remarkably, two-fifths of the varieties are native and rarely found elsewhere, giving Swiss wine a distinct identity. The greatest concentration is in Valais, where indigenous varieties account for nearly 30 percent of all vines. Some vineyards are over 35 years old, with a few surpassing 100 years; wines from these ancient vines may be labelled 'Vieilles Vignes' or 'Alte Reben'. Swiss winemakers play a vital role in preserving these rare and often endangered grapes.

It's not uncommon for a single producer to cultivate 20 or more varieties, a practice that reflects the country's diverse soils and microclimates. This also stems from Switzerland's historic self-sufficiency: as wine imports were limited, growers cultivated a wide range of grapes by necessity.

Swiss grape varieties fall into four categories:

Native Indigenous grapes unique to Switzerland. They account for almost 40 percent of all vines.

Traditional Non-native varieties with a history of over 100 years in Switzerland. They make up over a third of the country's vineyards.

International Globally recognized grapes introduced in the 20th century. They now account for around 16 percent of total plantings.

Novel New varieties created in Switzerland with enhanced attributes such as colour, taste or disease resistance. They are planted in around 10% of Swiss vineyards.

In the listing below recommended wines are shown after each grape variety. In addition, **Swiss wines to look out for** (pp66-73) profiles 18 of the best wines.

Native white grapes

Chasselas

The signature white grape of Switzerland and the second most planted variety (after Pinot Noir), Chasselas is key to the country's wine identity. Originating in the Lake Geneva region, it accounts for nearly 60% of the vineyards in Vaud. Known by different names – Fendant in Valais, Perlan in Geneva, Gutedel and Edelweiss in the German-speaking Region – it produces light, low-acidity wines with delicate flavours. Chasselas expresses its terroir remarkably well. Wines grown on granite soils are more floral, while limestone imparts fruity notes. Clay soils give the wine more weight, while the prime Dézaley slopes in Lavaux produce mineral-rich wines with remarkable depth. In Valais, the grape yields powerful wines with a pleasant bitterness, while Geneva's versions are fresh and fruity with a subtle fizz. The Three Lakes region produces wines with a flinty finish.

Though typically enjoyed young, Chasselas can age for a decade or more, developing complex nutty, honeyed flavours. It is a universally popular aperitif wine and a versatile food wine.

Recommended wines
Valais Domaine Cornulus, Clos du Mangold Fendant Vieilles Vignes
Vaud Massy Vins, Chemin de Fer Dézaley Grand Cru AOC
Three Lakes Cru de l'Hôpital, Chasselas de Fichillien

Petite Arvine

First mentioned over 400 years ago, Arvine (as it is sometimes called) is the emblematic white variety of Valais. Representing just over five percent of the region's vineyards, it has grown in popularity over the past two decades and is now among the most celebrated of Swiss white wine grapes.

Petite Arvine's hallmark is its lively acidity, along with aromas of citrus (especially pink grapefruit), pineapple and rhubarb – and a characteristic salty finish. Sweet, late-harvest versions labelled *flétri* (referring to the shrivelled grapes) have an enchanting bouquet of candied orange, honey and exotic spices, with a rich, lingering aftertaste.

Recommended wines
Valais Dry – Cave Valentin Andrei, Petite Arvine; Sweet – Domaine Chappaz, Petite Arvine Grain par Grain

Amigne

Three-quarters of this variety is grown in the village of Vétroz in Valais. First mentioned in 1686, 'Amigne de Vétroz' is a source of local pride even though it's grown in tiny quantities (it covers less than one percent of the Valais vineyards). The labels use a unique system of bees to indicate sweetness: one bee for dry, two for semi-sweet and three for sweet. Dry Amigne has flavours of vibrant mandarin and orange zest combined with crisp acidity and a slight tannic grip. The late-harvest dessert wines, enhanced by noble rot, develop golden hues and complex aromas of orange marmalade, honey and vanilla along with smooth, caramel flavours.

Recommended wines
Valais Semi-sweet – Les Celliers de Vétroz, Amigne; Sweet – Domaine Jean-René Germanier, Mitis Amigne de Vétroz Réserve

Räuschling

This medieval grape from the Rhine Valley was once cultivated in parts of Germany, Alsace and Switzerland. Today, it survives almost exclusively in Zürich, representing under four percent of the canton's vineyards. Räuschling produces light, dry wines with vibrant citrus notes and piercing acidity, making them particularly refreshing. With age they develop greater complexity, becoming more Riesling-like with honeyed and mineral nuances.

Recommended wine
German-speaking Region Weingut Pircher, Räuschling, Zürich

Humagne

One of Switzerland's oldest varieties, Humagne dates back to 1313. It is exclusive to Valais, where it covers a mere 26ha (64 acres) – a tiny proportion of the vineyard area. Nearly extinct by the early 20th century, it was rescued by determined winemakers. When Humagne Rouge (to which it is unrelated) appeared around 1900, the word 'Blanc' or 'Blanche' was added to Humagne to avoid confusion.

Humagne wines are elegant and fruity in their youth, with a powerful floral bouquet and lively acidity. With age, they evolve into rich, opulent wines with greater depth. Once known as *le vin des accouchées* ('new mothers' wine'), Humagne was believed to have high iron content and was traditionally given to women after childbirth for its supposed health benefits – a myth later disproven by modern science.

Recommended wine
Valais Domaine des Muses, Humagne Blanche Tradition

Completer

This ancient variety from Graubünden was first documented in 1321. Its name derives from 'completorium', the Benedictine monks' final prayer service of the day (known

Late-harvest Completer just beginning to be affected by botrytis (noble rot)

as compline), during which the monks were allowed a glass of wine – to be sipped in silence. This late-ripening grape benefits from the warm Alpine *föhn* wind, allowing it to be harvested as late as November when the grapes begin to shrivel on the vine. Completer produces rich, dry wines with quince, ripe apple, plum and honey notes reminiscent of a sweet wine. Its naturally high acidity gives the wines exceptional ageing potential, often for decades. Thanks to a small group of committed producers, this rare variety has made a comeback and now grows in 9ha (22 acres) of Graubünden's vineyards.

Recommended wine
German-speaking Region Weingut Wegelin, Completer Malanserrebe, Graubünden

Rèze

First mentioned in 1313, Rèze was once one of the most widely planted grapes in Valais. However, it was gradually replaced by more productive varieties and now covers just 5ha (12 acres) of the region. The wines have distinctive gooseberry and green apple aromas, with a crisp, resinous acidity. Rèze is famously associated with *Vin des glaciers*, a traditional wine aged in high-altitude cellars, which imparts distinct oxidative characteristics (see pp28-29).

Recommended wine
Valais Histoire d'Enfer, Rèze L'Enfer du Schiste

Silvaner (Johannisberg) vineyards, Chamoson, Valais

Native red grapes
Cornalin

The original red wine grape of Valais, Cornalin is properly called Rouge du Pays (or Landroter) and originated just over the Alps in the Aosta Valley in Italy. Now extinct in its native region, it thrives in Valais where it covers six percent of the vineyards. It was nearly abandoned in the 20th century but was revived in 1972 and misleadingly renamed 'Cornalin' (after Cornalin d'Aoste, an unrelated Italian variety – see Humagne Rouge p62). The deep cherry-coloured wines offer aromas of black cherries, raspberries and violets, with silky tannins and a pleasant bitterness. The grape's ability to age gracefully adds to its growing reputation as one of Switzerland's top red varieties.

Recommended wine
Valais Cave Maurice Zufferey, Cornalin

Traditional white grapes
Silvaner

Known locally as Johannisberg, Silvaner is an Austrian grape also grown in Germany and Alsace. It arrived in Valais in the mid-19th century and became one of the region's signature white varieties. About 100 years ago, the local name Johannisberg, previously used for Riesling, was rather

confusingly reassigned to Silvaner. Today, it is the second most important white grape in Valais, and comes in dry, medium-sweet and sweet styles.

Recommended wines
Valais Dry – Domaine Jean-René Germanier, Johannisberg de Chamoson; Sweet – Domaine du Mont d'Or, Johannisberg 'Saint-Martin'

Savagnin Blanc

Best known as the grape used in the French Jura to make Vin Jaune, Savagnin Blanc was first recorded in Valais in the late 16th century. It goes by different names: Heida in Upper Valais and Païen (meaning 'heathen', 'pagan' or 'old') in Lower Valais. In the Three Lakes region, it is labelled Traminer, as it belongs to the grape family of the same name that includes the aromatic Gewürztraminer. Savagnin Blanc produces full-bodied, well-structured dry wines with citrus, orange zest, apricot and quince notes.

Recommended wines
Valais Cave Caloz, Païen/Heida

Marsanne

Originating in France's Rhône Valley, Marsanne earned a reputation for creating long-lived, full-bodied wines. It arrived in Valais in the mid-19th century, where it became known locally as Ermitage, inspired by the French appellation Hermitage. In Switzerland, it is grown almost exclusively in Valais. As a dry wine, it has aromas of wild strawberries, raspberries, peach and apricot, while oak ageing adds almond nuttiness and smoky notes. When the grapes are left to hang on the vine to concentrate the grape sugars and harvested late (in December or even early January), they produce sweet, unctuous, opulent wines with an enticing rich gold colour.

Recommended wines
Valais Dry – Domaine Gérald Besse, Ermitage Vieille Vigne Les Serpentines; Sweet – Domaine des Muses, Polymnie 'Séduction Or' (Marsanne, Pinot Gris)

Pressing Pinot Noir in a 16th-century beam press, Schlossgut Bachtobel, Weinfelden, Thurgau

Traditional red grapes

Pinot Noir

Switzerland is the eighth-largest producer of Pinot Noir in the world, ahead of Chile and almost equal with Australia. It is the country's leading variety, representing a quarter of the vines overall and more than half of the German-speaking Region, where it is often labelled Blauburgunder.

Pinot Noir thrives in Switzerland's cooler climates, producing elegant, high-quality, single-varietal wines. Notable locations include the Bündner Herrschaft (Graubünden), Zürich, Thurgau and Schaffhausen areas of the German-speaking Region. In the Three Lakes region, it is used both for fine reds and for the rosé *Oeil de Perdrix* ('eye of the partridge'), which is known for its delicate salmon-pink hue and fruity profile. In Valais and Vaud, Pinot Noir is also blended with Gamay to create the easy-drinking Dôle (Valais) and Salvagnin (Vaud). These blends are light-bodied, with red fruit flavours and soft tannins.

Recommended wines
Valais Histoire d'Enfer, Pinot Noir L'Enfer du Calcaire
Vaud Domaine Henri Cruchon, Raisennaz Grand Cru
Three Lakes Caves de Chambleau, Cuvée Charlotte
German-speaking Region Studach Weinbau, Malanser Pinot Noir, Graubünden; Weingut Pircher, Pinot Noir Sélection Stadtberg, Zurich; Baumann Weingut, Pinot Noir Auslese, Schaffhausen

Gamay

Gamay first appeared in the first half of the 19th century and now accounts for over seven percent of Swiss vineyards, with most plantings in Valais, Vaud and Geneva. The style ranges from light, fruity wines with low tannins, best enjoyed young, to deeper, peppery wines aged in oak that deliver greater complexity. In Geneva, the grape is also used in the *Esprit de Genève* blend, which typically consists of half Gamay and at least two other red varieties, such as Gamaret, Garanoir, Syrah or Merlot. In Vaud's Lavaux subregion, a genetic mutation of Gamay known as Plant Robert (or Robez/Robaz) is grown.

Recommended wines
Valais Cave Christophe Abbet, Gamay de Fully Vieilles Vignes
Vaud Domaine Blaise Duboux, Plant Robez
Geneva Domaine de la Vigne Blanche, L'Esprit de Genève (Gamay, Gamaret, Cabernet Sauvignon)

Humagne Rouge

Humagne Rouge, a traditional Valais variety, is in fact Cornalin d'Aoste from Italy's Aosta Valley. It crossed the border around 1900 and is now cultivated almost exclusively in Valais. Humagne Rouge wines are rustic and expressive, with aromas of wild fruits, wooded undergrowth, bark and violets. When young, they have fresh, fruity flavours; with age, the wines become more structured and develop notes of pepper and woodsmoke.

Recommended wine
Valais Cave La Romaine, Humagne Rouge Les Empereurs

International white grapes

Chardonnay

This highly adaptable grape is grown in all six wine regions of Switzerland. Although it makes up less than three percent of vineyards, it is significant in Geneva and Three Lakes for sparkling wines, and in the German-speaking Region and Ticino for oak-aged single-varietals.

Recommended wines
German-speaking Region Weingut Roman Hermann, Chardonnay Grand Maître, Graubünden

Geneva Sparkling – La Cave de Genève, Baccarat Brut Blanc de Blancs

Pinot Gris

A grey-skinned mutation of Pinot Noir, this variety goes by different names: Malvoisie in Valais, Grauburgunder in the German-speaking Region and Pinot Gris in other French-speaking areas. It produces rich, aromatic dry wines and elegant sweet wines, particularly in Valais.

Recommended wine
Three Lakes Dry – Anne-Claire Schott, Pinot Gris

Sauvignon Blanc

Originating from France's Loire Valley, Sauvignon Blanc is now planted across Switzerland. It first appeared in Geneva, but the German-speaking Region – notably Zürich, Aargau and Graubünden – has since surpassed Geneva in plantings. Swiss Sauvignon Blanc leans stylistically towards New Zealand's aromatic green and tropical fruits rather than France's more delicate mineral-driven expression.

Recommended wine
Geneva Domaine de la Comtesse Eldegarde, Sauvignon Blanc

International red grapes

Merlot

The second most important red grape in Switzerland, Merlot first appeared in Vaud in the mid-19th century. Its greatest success by far is in Ticino where, having been introduced in 1906 after the devastating phylloxera crisis, it now dominates. Benefitting from the Mediterranean, sub-Alpine climate, Merlot makes wines that range from light, crowd-pleasing reds to rich, oaked varieties. In Ticino, up to a quarter of the Merlot harvest is used to make white wines. In the other Swiss regions, it appears as either single-varietal wines or blends with local or international varieties.

Recommended wines
Geneva La Cave de Genève, Les Vins de Philippe Chevrier Merlot-Cabernet Sauvignon
Ticino Gialdi Vini, Sassi Grossi

Syrah

Four-fifths of all the Syrah in Switzerland is in Valais, where it was introduced from France's Rhône Valley after World War I. Several of the vineyards are over 60 years old and still related to the original stock. The wines have bold flavours of ripe blackberries, blackcurrants, woodsmoke and spices like pepper and liquorice. The finest examples are aged in French oak, developing complex aromas of game and leather.

Recommended wine
Valais Simon Maye et Fils, Syrah Vieilles Vignes

Novel white grapes

Müller-Thurgau

Dr Hermann Müller from the Swiss canton of Thurgau developed this variety in Germany in the late 19th century. Originally believed to be a cross between Riesling and Silvaner (and still called 'Riesling-Silvaner'), later research revealed its true parentage: Riesling and the lesser-known Madeleine Royale. Though once dismissed for producing unremarkable wines, Swiss producers have elevated this grape to make fresh, citrus-driven wines with lively acidity. It is now Switzerland's second most planted white grape – around three percent of the vineyards.

Recommended wine
German-speaking Region Michael Broger Weinbau, Müller-Thurgau Ottenberg, Thurgau

Doral

With Chasselas and Chardonnay as its parents, Doral has more aromatic intensity, acidity and body than Chasselas, plus notes of citrus and apricot. For the past 20 years, Doral has been used to create small quantities of intriguing single-varietal wines, primarily in Vaud.

Recommended wine
Vaud Cave de la Côte, Doral Expression

Novel red grapes
Gamaret

A rising star in Swiss viticulture, Gamaret is a combination of Gamay and the white variety Reichensteiner. Though it was only introduced in 1990, it has already become Switzerland's fourth most planted red grape, mainly in Vaud, Geneva and Valais. Its wines exhibit deep purple hues, spicy aromas, ripe black fruit flavours and firm tannins. Gamaret is also valued for adding depth to blends and shines in oak-aged single-varietal wines.

Recommended wine
Geneva Domaine du Clos des Pins, Gamaret Mandragore

Garanoir

Created alongside Gamaret from the same parents, Garanoir is fruitier and less spicy with lower acidity. It is mostly used in blends for its colour and tannins, though some oak-aged single-varietal wines are starting to appear.

Recommended wine
Vaud Château Le Rosey, Garanoir Premier Grand Cru

Diolinoir

The original idea behind this grape was to create a version of Pinot Noir with greater colour that could help beef up red wine blends. In production since 1998, Diolinoir wines are inky-dark in colour with notes of blackberries, cherries and violets, supported by smooth, firm tannins. Mainly grown in Valais, Diolinoir is increasingly used for single-varietal wines that can age for 15-20 years. Its parents are Pinot Noir and Robin Noir (originally called Rouge de Diolly, named after the Valais village where it was discovered).

Recommended wine
Valais Provins, Diolinoir Domaine de l'Évêché

Swiss wines to look out for

It's a challenge to pick the best wines from Switzerland's vast diversity of regions, producers and grape varieties. Here we highlight stand-out examples of the main grape varieties in all six regions and just one wine per producer (even if several of their wines are worthy of attention). While some are produced in quantity, others are harder to get hold of: if they are not available in the shops, look out for them on restaurant wine lists, or you could go direct to the winery.

Martin Donatsch of Domaine Donatsch

Valais white

Cave Benoît Dorsaz, Petite Arvine de Fully Quintessence

Benoît, the fifth generation of a winemaking family, is a Petite Arvine specialist. He makes three versions: dry unoaked, late-harvest sweet and this dry oaked Quintessence. The result is stunning: intense aromas of citrus peel, stone and tropical fruits, and granite lead to a rich, elegant, full-bodied palate and a signature saltiness on the slightly tannic finish. Any residual oakiness vanishes with age – though in this case it's hard to wait.

Domaine Chappaz, Grain Ermitage (Marsanne)

Marie-Thérèse Chappaz is a Swiss wine icon who has been working wonders since 1988. Her wines are some of the most sought-after both in Switzerland and abroad, especially the sweet ones. Her vineyards on precipitous terraced slopes exemplify heroic Alpine viticulture. The astonishing Grain Ermitage is made from 100-year-old Marsanne vines. It has a rich golden hue, a complex nose of tropical fruits with floral and stony notes, a spicy, vanilla flavour and juicy acidity on the palate and a salty touch on the finish. It can age for at least 30 years.

St Jodern Kellerei, Heida Veritas (Savagnin Blanc)

St Jodern in Visperterminen (see p123) is a cooperative with hundreds of members owning minute plots who work together mainly at weekends. This village is home to some of the highest vineyards in Europe: planted on moraine and slate, many are well over 100 years old. The Savagnin Blanc grape, called Heida in these parts, accounts for almost one-third of the cooperative's production. Veritas, produced in small quantities, is the pinnacle of the range.

Aromas of ripe stone and exotic fruits with floral notes and crushed stones make an intense first impression. The wine is full-bodied with fresh acidity and alcohol on the high side. The finish is powerful and persistent with a saline character.

Valais red

Domaine Jean-René Germanier, Cayas Réserve Syrah du Valais

The flagship wine of this million-bottle producer is a pure Syrah called Cayas. Some 30,000 bottles are produced each year, making it one of the most widely available Swiss fine wines. It is made by third- and fourth-generation owners and winemakers, Gilles Besse and his uncle, Jean-René Germanier. Aged for 24 months in French *barriques* (half of them new), Cayas has a classic Syrah profile of dark berries, liquorice, cloves, pepper, violets and chocolate. Powerful, elegant and fresh, with fine tannins and a long, intense finish, it can age for up to 20 years.

Denis Mercier, Cornalin

Over 40 years ago Denis and Anne-Cathérine Mercier took over the vineyards that used to belong to the Mercier family castle, perched on a craggy outcrop above Sierre. Daughter Madeleine joined them in 2012 after working in Ticino, Oregon and at Opus One in California. Father Denis helped to rediscover the Cornalin variety and revive its fortunes. The Mercier rendition of this now iconic regional grape is one of the very best. A fruity, floral, spicy nose is followed by ripe red and black fruits on the palate with juicy acidity and a fruity, spicy finish. The tannins soften nicely over 10 to 15 years.

Vaud white

Domaine La Colombe, Brez Grand Cru (Chasselas)

Laura Paccot, the fourth generation to manage the estate, is building on her father Raymond's pioneering role as a

biodynamic producer. La Colombe's range includes five single-vineyard Chasselas wines, each with different terroir. The Brez site in Féchy, La Côte is planted with almost 50-year-old vines growing in deep chalky soil with chunky gravel. The resulting wine is intense yet delicate, with aromas of ripe fruits, flowers and herbs leading to a vibrant, refreshing palate and a salty finish. Brez rewards patience and can age well for 15 to 20 years.

Domaine Blaise Duboux, Haut de Pierre Vieilles Vignes Dézaley Grand Cru (Chasselas)

Blaise is the 17th generation at the helm of the family estate in Epesses, Lavaux. This remarkably powerful wine, from 35-year-old vines that grow on the seemingly vertical slopes of Dézaley, reflects his reverence for the Chasselas grape. The wine has complex aromas of ripe citrus and stone fruits with spicy notes and a dense, complex palate with a saline touch on the long finish; it has great potential for ageing.

Domaine de la Pierre Latine, Clos du Crosex Grillé 'Cuvée des Immortels' Aigle Grand Cru (Chasselas)

Winston Churchill, whose ancestors owned this estate for nearly 100 years, used to exchange boxes of cigars for bottles of wine and visited the estate in 1946 on his victory tour through Europe. *Crosex Grillé* translates as 'sun trap' and the south-facing amphitheatre of this single vineyard in Yvorne, Chablais explains why. With the added benefit of low rainfall and the warming *föhn* wind, the grapes ripen perfectly. The result is a full-bodied wine possessing aromas of citrus and apple with floral notes, quince and honey, and a salty-mineral character on the rich, lingering finish.

Vaud red

Les Frères Dutruy, Les Romaines Gamaret Grande Réserve

Brothers Christian and Julien Dutruy are the fourth generation to manage this estate in Founex, La Côte, having taken over from their father almost 20 years ago. Christian worked in Napa Valley and South Africa, while Julien studied oenology in Bordeaux and interned in Burgundy, Alsace and New Zealand. The grapes from older vines on their best sites of clay and limestone soils go into the premium line of 'Les Romaines', all matured in oak for at least a year. This Gamaret has aromas of ripe black fruits as well as black pepper and toast. Full-bodied with smooth tannins and a savoury finish.

Geneva white

Domaine Les Hutins, Sauvignon Barrique 1er Cru Coteaux de Dardagny

The Hutin family was actively involved in the renaissance of the Geneva wine region and the establishment of the Geneva AOC in the 1980s. The estate is now managed by the fifth generation and cultivates a wide range of varieties. Sauvignon Blanc stands out in both the unoaked version and this oaked variant. Made from 40-year-old vines, its powerful acidity and high alcohol are well integrated, with aromas of tropical fruits.

Geneva red

Domaine Grand'Cour, Grand'Cour (Cabernets Franc and Sauvignon, Merlot)

Jean-Pierre Pellegrin is a star in the Geneva region: since he took over the estate in Peissy from his father more than 30 years ago, he has led efforts to shift the region's focus from quantity to quality. This Grand'Cour Bordeaux

blend is one of his legendary wines, aged for 24 months in Burgundy barrels. The nose is wonderfully complex with dark berry, tobacco, spicy and savoury aromas, and there's a smoky oakiness on the full-bodied palate.

Three Lakes red

Domaine de la Maison Carrée, Auvernier Pinot Noir

Owned and managed by the Perrochet family for nearly 200 years, the estate is now run by Alexandre, who trained in Burgundy and other regions of Switzerland. Two old vertical wooden presses are still in use, while the approach to winemaking is rooted in modern science. The vineyards, half of which are planted with Pinot Noir, slope down to Lake Neuchâtel. Auvernier is aged in mainly large wooden barrels as well as smaller oak barrels. Powerful aromas of red berries and floral notes, a fruity, medium-bodied palate with well-integrated acidity and fine tannins, lead to a long, fresh finish with a slight salty touch.

German-speaking Region white

Schwarzenbach Weinbau, Räuschling Seehalden

Alain Schwarzenbach is the fifth generation to manage the family estate on the Gold Coast of Lake Zürich. He has worked in Australia and New Zealand, and his wife Marilen has spent time in Italy and Tasmania. The estate is credited with reviving the ancient Räuschling grape, from which it now produces three different wines, including this Räuschling Seehalden. Meaning 'lakeside slopes', this single vineyard is planted on deep, weathered sandstone, and produces an elegant wine with notes of lemon, blood orange, apple and exotic fruits, tingling acidity and flinty aromas. Capable of ageing for 20 years.

Domaine Donatsch, Completer 'Malanserrebe'

Martin Donatsch took over the estate in Malans, Graubünden in 2001 from his late father Thomas, who revolutionized winemaking in the Bündner Herrschaft area. Martin makes outstanding Chardonnay and Pinot Noir as well as this fine Completer, a rare, high-acid variety dating from the 14th century and rescued from oblivion at the end of the 20th. The grapes are harvested late in mid-November, but the wine is vinified dry and aged for one year in used oak barrels. It is fruity, floral, nutty and yeasty on the nose, full-bodied with lively acidity, slight sweetness and a nice tannic touch on the long, velvety finish. Thanks to the phenomenal acidity, this wine can age for 30 years plus.

German-speaking Region red
Schlossgut Bachtobel, Pinot Noir N°3

Family-owned since 1784, this historic estate in Thurgau is now managed by Johannes Meier, the eighth generation. The majority of its production is Pinot Noir, of which there are four cuvées, handily numbered from one to four. No 3, the estate's most important wine, comes from vines over 35 years old, processed in two massive oak presses dating from 1584 and 1729 and matured for 15 months in Burgundy barrels. Concentrated berry fruit aromas, a silky texture and a lingering finish make it approachable after about four years but it can age for 10-15 years.

Weingut Fromm, Pinot Noir Selvenen

Georg Fromm has a reputation for making sensational Pinot Noir in Malans, Graubünden (and previously in the Marlborough region of New Zealand), and son Marco is now actively involved at the estate. Of their five single-vineyard Pinot Noir wines, Selvenen is the largest and most readily available. Produced mainly from vines over 50 years old, the wine is aged for around one year in Burgundy barrels. Refined and intense on the nose with firm tannins on the palate, it has real depth of flavour, can be enjoyed after about five years and promises some 20 years of ageing.

Ticino white

Tenuta Castello di Morcote, Castello di Morcote Bianco (Merlot, Chardonnay)

The ruins of the Duke of Milan's 15th-century fortress in Vico Morcote are monumental evidence of this estate's rich history. Surrounded by terraced vineyards overlooking Lake Lugano, it has been transformed over the last 15 years by the third generation of the Gianini family, with a new cellar, restaurant and accommodation. While its Merlot Riserva red wines are amongst the best in the region, the white Merlot – one of Ticino's surprises – is also a leading example. This Bianco del Merlot has a dash of Chardonnay for added richness. Aged in French oak for at least a year, it's elegant and full-bodied with intense aromas of ripe citrus and yellow stone fruits, lively acidity and an invitingly long, creamy, mineral finish.

Ticino red

Azienda Agricola Zündel, Orrizonte (Merlot, Cabernet Sauvignon)

Over the past 40 years Christian Zündel – from the German-speaking Region – has realized his dream of making world-class Merlot in Ticino. His daughter Myra, who trained in Italy and Switzerland, took over in 2020. Orrizonte is produced from probably the oldest Merlot vineyard in Ticino, first planted in 1905; it's considered the wine that established Zündel's reputation. Aged in Burgundy barrels for 12-18 months, with about 10% Cabernet Sauvignon, it's medium-bodied with a silky texture, aromas of plum, cherry and herb – approachable in its youth but capable of long ageing.

Fromage that formed a nation

Switzerland's cheese story goes back to the Iron Age. Archaeological digs on the shores of Lake Neuchâtel have uncovered Celtic pottery shards with residue curds, proving cheese existed long before the rebellion of William Tell in the 14th century. The Romans noted the creamy delights of *Caseus Helveticus* (a precursor to Sbrinz), earning it a mention in Pliny the Elder's writings.

By the Middle Ages, cheese was central to Swiss life, especially in isolated Alpine villages. It wasn't just food; it could be currency – it was sometimes used in lieu of rent or to pay taxes. By the 19th century, there were more than 1,000 cheese varieties, but that diversity wouldn't last. Powerful dairy cooperatives – dubbed the 'Cheese Mafia' – imposed strict controls, curbing the number to around 700 today. While their regulations erased many regional cheese styles, they also played a role in nation-building. In the 1950s, surplus milk was pragmatically channelled into fondue, helping it to become Switzerland's most beloved dish.

The distinct Alpine pastures of Switzerland are the secret to its cheese. Cows, goats, and sheep graze on meadows rich with over 450 plant species, from edelweiss to gentian and pansies. These infuse the milk with complex, subtle flavours. At lower altitudes, the taste is buttery and creamy. Climb higher, and you'll find earthy mushroom notes shifting to floral tones. Slope exposure, season, and ripening time all add to the nuance. As cheese expert Eddy Baillifard (see p172) explains, 'the sheer variety of plants at high altitudes creates a signature taste no factory can replicate.'

Switzerland produces around 200,000 tonnes of cheese annually, using nearly half of the country's milk supply; cows' milk accounts for 99 percent of all cheese production. So revered are Swiss bovines that every autumn, during the *Désalpe* or *Alpabzug* (when the cows return from mountain pastures), they're adorned in colourful regalia with gigantic cowbells and paraded through the village to the cheers of onlookers.

After chocolate, cheese is the second-largest food export, with over 79,000 tonnes shipped in 2024. To further safeguard this heritage, Switzerland established the AOP (*Appellation d'Origine Protégée*) system in 2000, which currently protects 12 distinct cheese styles – stipulating, for example, that every cheese must be made within 20km (12.5 miles) of the farm. From the Gruyère of Fribourg to the Emmental of Bern, every variety reflects its region, environment and the passion of its artisans.

Ten of the best Swiss cheeses

There are an estimated 1,300 mountain pastures in Switzerland used for cheese production. Gruyère really is the big cheese, but it simply sits at the pinnacle of an incredibly rich, complex and varied offering.

Berner Alpkäse AOP & Berner Hobelkäse AOP	Made in the high pastures of the Bernese Alps, following a recipe dating back to 1872. Berner Alpkäse develops a golden hue, rich aroma and bold, spicy flavours.
Bleuchâtel	From Neuchâtel, this is Switzerland's original blue cheese. Creamy yet punchy flavours, it is likened to both Roquefort and Stilton, but with its own Alpine character.
Caramel Gruyère	This rebel Gruyère is the work of renowned cheesemaker Jacques Duttweiler. Aged for 32 months in mountain cellars rich with natural molasses, it crumbles into golden shards that melt like toffee.
Emmentaler AOP	Possibly the definitive Swiss cheese, Emmentaler AOP has captured global attention. Its famous holes are formed when tiny specks of hay in the milk trigger bacteria to release carbon dioxide.
Mont Vully	This ivory-gold cheese from Fribourg has a special ingredient that gives it an alluring aroma and a taste which is both delicate and subtly spicy. Aged for at least 10 weeks in Pinot Noir.
Raclette du Valais AOP	Raclette, from the French verb *racler*, meaning 'to scrape', has been a fixture in Valais since the 16th century. Legend has it that it was conceived by a herdsman when his cheese melted near the embers of a fire. Naturally lactose-free.
Sbrinz AOP	The godfather of Swiss cheese – aged for 22 months to develop a deep, nutty intensity. Made exclusively from the milk of the Swiss Brown Cow. Extra-hard, it's the original mountain snack.
Tête de Moine AOP	Created by monks in Bellelay Abbey in Bern, it was first documented in 1790, and used as currency to pay taxes. Aged up to 100 days, it isn't sliced but shaved with a *girolle* into delicate rosettes, releasing its melt-in-the-mouth creaminess.
Tomme Vaudoise	A soft, creamy cheese with aromas of fresh milk and curd that becomes runnier as it ripens. Tomme can be found in many parts of *Suisse Romande* and neighbouring France.
Zincarlin	Ticino's mini mountain-shaped cheese, Zincarlin, is a rare gem crafted by hand from a blend of raw cow's and goat's milk. Aged versions develop a bold, tangy depth.

Wine events and other festivals

From boisterous carnivals and fancy dress parades evoking the country's eclectic origins, to tastings and cellar visits, the Swiss year is packed with memorable events for you to organize your holiday around. For 'Open Cellar' events across Switzerland, see the end of this chapter.

Fête des Vignerons, Vevey (see p15)

With four national languages and wildly different ways of marking the seasons, Switzerland resists easy definition. Its annual events are much the same – steeped in tradition, rich in ritual and often delightfully idiosyncratic. From Zürich's flaming snowman and sausage-fuelled saints' days in Lavaux to chocolate cauldrons, onion garlands and lakeside jazz, each festival is deeply local yet warmly open to visitors. Whether it's a folkloric frenzy or a joyous cellar crawl, the common ingredients are authenticity, seasonal flavour and a generous dose of intrigue. More often than not, wine oils the wheels – so open your mind, loosen your belt and enjoy cracking the cultural code of this multi-faceted Alpine nation.

January
Du Villette et c'est la fête, Aran, VD

Fête du Villette, Aran

On the last Saturday in January the wine village of Aran holds a special event to honour the patron saint of winemakers: Saint Vincent. In true Vaudois fashion, not only does the wine flow freely but so do the sausages. Known locally as *Papet Vaudois*, this pork sausage stuffed with cabbage and spices has become a symbol of cantonal pride. Close to 1,000 of these bangers are dished out during the day. Live music further lubricates the festivities.

caveau-villette.ch

Non Filtré, Neuchâtel, NE

For more than 50 years this unique event has been going strong in Neuchâtel. It all began in the 1970s when a winemaker ran out of wine for a wedding party and decided to draw young, unracked Chasselas from the barrel for the thirsty

Non Filtré

Morgestraich, Basel

revellers. Now, every January, local winemakers get together to celebrate all things unfiltered. Held in various locations in central Neuchâtel. Tickets can be bought online.

neuchatelvinsterroir.ch

February
Fasnacht, various locations

This folkloric festival, rooted in pre-Lent traditions, banishes winter's icy grasp with an explosion of colour, chaos and odd characters. The Morgestraich in Basel is a surreal lantern-lit dawn parade, while in Valais the eerie Child Catcher of Lötschental and wild-eyed Tschäggättä beasts chase (often tipsy) onlookers. Between confetti storms, brass bands and float parades, locals keep the revelry alive with hearty Swiss reds. Wherever you are, with Fasnacht there's never a dull moment: it's a three-day, wine-fuelled fever dream.

Tschäggättä, Lötschental

myswitzerland.com

March

Festin Neuchâtelois, Neuchâtel, NE

This communal dining concept brings together foodies for an all-out feast for the senses. The one-day event features special menus from more than 30 of the region's restaurants, pairing local wines with signature flavours. More than 10,000 diners take part each year, so bookings are essential. Restaurant menus can be found online.

festin-neuchatelois.ch

April

Cully Jazz, Cully, VD

Montreux is synonymous with its legendary Jazz Festival, but a cool alternative runs every April on the idyllic shores of Cully, at the foot of the Lavaux vineyards. Running over 10 days, the international festival serves up soulful tunes and avant-garde acts in numerous venues – including wine cellars and cafés – throughout the village. There are plenty of pop-up bars featuring wines primarily from Lavaux and the trains run until late.

cullyjazz.ch

Cully Jazz

Sechseläuten Festival

Divinum, Morges, VD

This week-long lakeside event is one of the largest in Switzerland, attracting thousands each year – they even offer a festival pass for the truly committed. Open till

Divinum

late, there are various pop-up restaurants to enjoy along with the more than 1,000 wines being poured from Switzerland and beyond. Tickets can be bought on-site and there's convenient access to public transport.

salon–divinum.ch

Sechseläuten Festival, Zürich, ZH

Every April, a towering snowman effigy called the *Böögg* (or Bogeyman) is set ablaze at exactly 6pm in Zürich's Sechseläutenplatz. Legend has it, the quicker his head explodes, the sunnier the summer days ahead. Adding to the gaiety are brass bands, costumed horsemen, guild parades and fireworks in this whacky spring rite that's been lighting up Zürich since the 16th century.

zuerich.com/en/events–nightlife/typical–events/sechselauten

Tracassets, Epesses, VD

Held every two years, the wine village of Epesses bursts into technicolour chaos for the *Championnat du Monde des Tracassets*. These motorized vineyard carts – usually found hauling grapes – get a flamboyant makeover and join a zany cavalcade through Lavaux; it's a village fête and motor show rolled into one. Expect outlandish designs, plenty of wine, food stands and more

Tracassets

than 15,000 spectators lining the vineyard paths. The next edition rolls in spring 2026. Arrive early for the best view.

tracassets.ch

May

Wein Promenade, Malans, GR

A family-friendly wine walk held around the quaint village of Malans. Dotted along the easy walking trail are some of the most famed

Wein Promenade

Mangialonga

Lavaux Classic

winemakers of the region, pouring samples of their best cuvées. Things conclude with a communal barbecue and live music, where everyone – including the winemakers – party till sunset. Tickets on-site, cash only.

weinpromenade.ch

Mangialonga, Mendrisiotto, TI

Every 1 May, Mendrisiotto transforms into a moving feast. This 10 km (6.2 mile) stroll winds through vineyards and villages with tasting stops that showcase local producers and seasonal specialities. It's a fiesta with a serious flavour – on average, 17,000 glasses of wine are poured throughout the day. This beloved tradition has limited spots and sells out fast, so be sure to book early.

vineriadeimir.ch/gli-eventi/

June
Lavaux Classic, Grandvaux, VD

Set against the picture-postcard backdrop of the Lavaux vineyards, Lavaux Classic offers a captivating blend of classical music and scenic charm. Over 10 days, intimate concerts are held in Cully, Grandvaux and Vevey. It's an atmospheric escape worth planning for, with free lakeside performances, rising star showcases and candlelit concerts.

lavauxclassic.ch

July
Marchés Folkloriques, Vevey, VD

From July to August, Vevey's town centre transforms into a vibrant celebration of Swiss tradition. The Marchés Folkloriques fill the historic square with the sounds of brass bands, yodellers, alphorn players and folk dancers. Take a leisurely stroll through the open-air market, pick up a unique souvenir glass and sample a rotating selection of local wines. Regional foods and crafts round out this festive showcase of Vaud's culture and community spirit, all against a backdrop of the Alps.

marchesfolkloriques.com

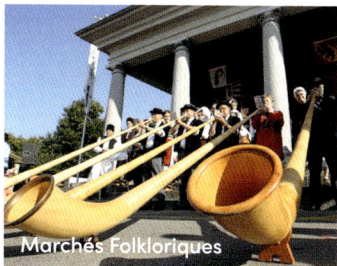

Marchés Folkloriques

August
Swiss Wine Grand Tasting, Zürich, ZH

A rare passport to Switzerland's most coveted wines, the Swiss Wine Grand Tasting is a revelation for curious wine connoisseurs. Here, the prestigious *Mémoire des Vins Suisses* winemakers unveil their most distinguished and aged vintages, seldom poured outside their cellars. Each sip is a taste of the unique Alpine terroirs and the artistry of Swiss viticulture. There is also the chance to enjoy the best wines from the vintage of 10 years ago during the annual Vintage Tasting. These events regularly sell out, so plan well in advance.

swiss-wine-tasting.ch

September
Fête des Vendanges, Lutry, VD and Neuchâtel, NE

This late-September celebration once marked the start of the harvest and was a pragmatic way to clear cellars of bottles. Now, partly due to climate change, it occurs near the end of harvest. One of the biggest wine parties of the year,

Lutry's lakeside carnival spans the entire weekend, with crowds gathering each night to enjoy wine, live music and a lively atmosphere in the village square. In Neuchâtel, highlights include the famous fireworks display and the *Grand Corso Fleuri* float parade.

Fête des Vendanges, Neuchâtel

fetedesvendanges.ch (Lutry)

fete-des-vendanges.ch (Neuchâtel)

October

La Fête de la Châtaigne, Fully, VS

Every October, more than 40,000 visitors gather in Fully to celebrate the chestnut harvest, known locally as *la Châtaigne*. The festival's bustling open-air market features hundreds of stalls selling traditional *brisolée* – freshly roasted chestnuts served with cheese, dried meat and

La Fête de la Châtaigne

autumn fruits – alongside other regional specialities. Wine lovers can explore the Village des Petites Arvines, sampling this iconic Valais white in various styles. Live music and family-friendly activities, including chestnut foraging in nearby groves, add to the festive autumn atmosphere.

fetedelachataigne.ch

Herbstfest, Hallau, SH

Every autumn, the medieval village of Hallau celebrates its centuries-old wine traditions. This lively festival showcases Schaffhausen's rich viticultural heritage, with costumed parades, folk music, tastings of the region's prized Pinot Noirs and more. Wander through the ancient streets, savouring rustic local cuisine with a glass of Räuschling. A joyous fusion of history, culture and harvest revelry, it's Schaffhausen at its most enchanting.

hallauer-herbstfest.ch

November
Expovina, Zürich, ZH

Zürich's two-week floating wine celebration has been a

Herbstfest

Expovina

staple since the 1950s. Classic 'wine ships' moored on Lake Zürich host hundreds of wine estates and retailers. All six Swiss wine regions are represented, along with a raft of international names. On land, a pop-up festival park dishes up food to match the fun. Tickets are available online.

expovina.ch

Zibelemärit Onion Festival, Bern, BE

Every year, 50,000 kg of onions fill Bern's old town, transforming the city into an aromatic arena that's not for the faint of heart.

The market opens at the crack of dawn and so do the festivities, including onion braiding, folk music and sampling onion pizza and *Chnoblibrot* (Bernese garlic bread). It's a pungent paradise that may not win you many friends, but you'll never look at onions the same way again.

Zibelemärit

bern.ch

L'Escalade

December

L'Escalade, Geneva, GE

The festival year rounds out with one of the quirkiest events. Geneva transforms into a festive battlefield – minus the swords, but with a lot of mulled wine. The escalade of Geneva's ramparts marks the city's 1602 triumph over the marauding Savoyards, famously foiled by a flying pot of hot soup. The city is ablaze with torchlit parades, costumed re-enactments and the smashing of chocolate cauldrons filled with marzipan treats. It's equal parts dramatic, delicious and delightfully boozy.

geneve.com

Regional Open Cellar Events

From May to June, Switzerland's winemakers throw open their cellar doors – and their bottles. Each of the six wine regions hosts its own edition of Caves Ouvertes (offene Weinkeller/Cantine aperte), some for a single day, others over a weekend. Visitors are invited to taste, meet producers and wander through vineyard-fringed villages in full spring bloom. These are lively, unpretentious gatherings – bring comfortable shoes, an empty glass and a thirst for discovery.

Valais

The Ascension weekend belongs to Valais. Three days, hundreds of wineries, and everything from Cornalin and Syrah to Petite Arvine and Chasselas's local moniker Fendant – all poured with gusto. Switzerland's largest wine region requires some forward planning – and stamina. Admission is free.

caves-ouvertes-valais.ch

Valais

Vaud

Over the Pentecost (Whitsun) long weekend, wineries across Vaud's six subregions open their doors. Lavaux's famous terraces draw crowds, but hidden gems abound. One of the most frequented cellar events, tickets (purchased online) include a special tasting glass, hat and free public transport throughout the weekend.

Vaud

mescavesouvertes.ch

Geneva

Geneva

Held on a Saturday in May, close to 80 wineries are open to visit. A ticket – pay by cash at any participating estate – includes a tasting glass and access to shuttle buses linking each subregion. Time is tight, so target one of the key wine areas: Jussy, Satigny or Lully.

geneveterroir.ch

Three Lakes

Held in May, this two-day event kicks off on Friday evening

Three Lakes

and runs through Saturday, with more than 40 cellar doors open for lakeside sipping. Shuttle buses link the charming villages, making it easy to explore this mini Burgundy of Swiss wine – think refreshing Chardonnays and elegant Pinot Noirs.

cavesouvertesneuchatel.ch

German-speaking Region

This diverse wine region stretches from the rolling valleys of Schaffhausen to the peaks of the Bündner Herrschaft. More than 200 winemakers welcome visitors

German-speaking Region

into their cellars, usually during the first weekend of May. Explore the various events and tastings using the interactive online map. Admission is usually free.

deutschschweizerwein.ch

Ticino

Switzerland's only wine region south of the Alps, Ticino's festival spans two weekends in May. Sopraceneri (north of Monte Ceneri) starts the event, followed by Sottoceneri's famed areas to the south like Lugano and Mendrisio. A Merlot lover's paradise – red or white. There are shuttle services from Bellinzona and Lugano.

cantineaperte.ch

Ticino

Getting around Switzerland: easy, scenic and stress-free

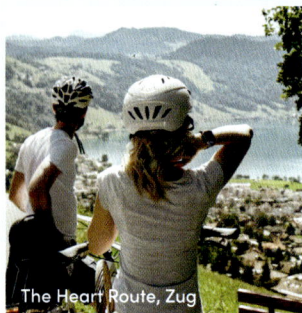

The Heart Route, Zug

Switzerland is one of the world's easiest countries to explore, thanks to its remarkably efficient and interconnected transport network. Whether you travel by train, car, bicycle, on foot or by boat, you'll find the Swiss system designed for seamless, carefree journeys – and spectacular scenery along the way.

The country's public transport network spans over 29,000km (18,000 miles) of rail, road and waterways, making it the densest transport network in the world. Trains, buses, and boats reach nearly every town and village, allowing travellers to venture far beyond the main tourist hubs with ease.

Swiss trains are world-famous for punctuality, cleanliness and comfort. The Swiss Travel System links trains, buses and boats into one cohesive network. The **Swiss Travel Pass** is the ultimate ticket for visitors, offering unlimited travel for 3, 4, 8 or 15 consecutive days, plus free or discounted entry to over 500 museums. You can buy the pass online, or at most train stations.

For those **renting a car,** driving in Switzerland is straightforward with well-maintained roads and clear signage. A special pass (called a **vignette** and costing CHF40, available online) is required to use

Paddle Steamer, Lake Luzern

GoldenPass Express, Rougemont, Vaud

motorways, and parking in city centres can be expensive – consider Park+Ride options outside major towns for an easy way in. Scenic drives like the Furka or Grimsel Pass offer some of Europe's most breathtaking views, perfect for confident drivers seeking adventure.

Cycling is another excellent way to experience Switzerland's varied landscapes. With over 12 national bike routes mapped by **SwitzerlandMobility**, travellers can ride through vineyards, alongside lakes or over Alpine passes. **E-bike rentals** are widely available and make hills far more manageable. Many trains allow you to bring bikes (with a separate bike ticket), making it easy to combine rail and cycling.

On foot, Switzerland is a hiker's paradise with more than 65,000km (40,000 miles) of well-marked trails, from easy valley strolls to challenging Alpine treks. Signposts make navigating straightforward, and combining hikes with mountain trains or lake boats can turn a simple walk into a memorable day out. Always check weather forecasts before setting off, especially in the mountains.

Speaking of lakes, **public boats** ply the waters of Lake Luzern, Lake Geneva, Lake Thun and many others. These ferries are part of the regular transport system – not just sightseeing cruises – and the Swiss Travel Pass covers them at no extra cost. Timetables vary by season, so check ahead.

For international arrivals or onward journeys, trains and buses connect directly at airports and border stations, with guaranteed connections throughout the network. Wherever you go, the Swiss Travel System ensures smooth connections, and with tickets like the Swiss Travel Pass, visitors can save significantly while enjoying one of the world's most beautiful and hassle-free transport networks. 🇨🇭

For more information visit **switzerland.com/tickets**.

Content supported by Switzerland Tourism

Wine routes

There are many ways to explore Switzerland. For some, hiking the high passes is the only option; for others, a cruise on the lake or a scenic railway journey is a must. Then there are e-bikes and balloon rides and of course a traditional motoring holiday... In this section we suggest eight routes using different modes of transport and covering all six wine regions.

Salgesch, Upper Valais

Sion, Lower Valais

ITINERARY 1

Valais: Lower Valais (Martigny to Vétroz and back)

Mode e-bike **Cycling time** 3 hours (excluding stops)
Distance 50km (31 miles) **Elevation gain:** 400m (1,312ft)

This cycle route through the heart of Valais delivers steep vineyards, medieval tales, sacred vines and enough wine stops to make you rethink your return time. You'll need power assistance to get you through – but the payoff is worth every pedal stroke.

Start in **Martigny**, where Publibike offers easy e-bike rentals directly from the train station. One person can hire up to five bikes (download and register on the app ahead of time). From here, head northeast across the river Rhône and on to **Route de Branson**. Keep the vineyards to your left and the river to your right. The route is mostly flat, with a few early inclines. Look out for tiny vine parcels clinging to the higher slopes – this is winemaking of the most vertical kind.

In under 30 minutes, you'll reach the wine village of **Fully**,

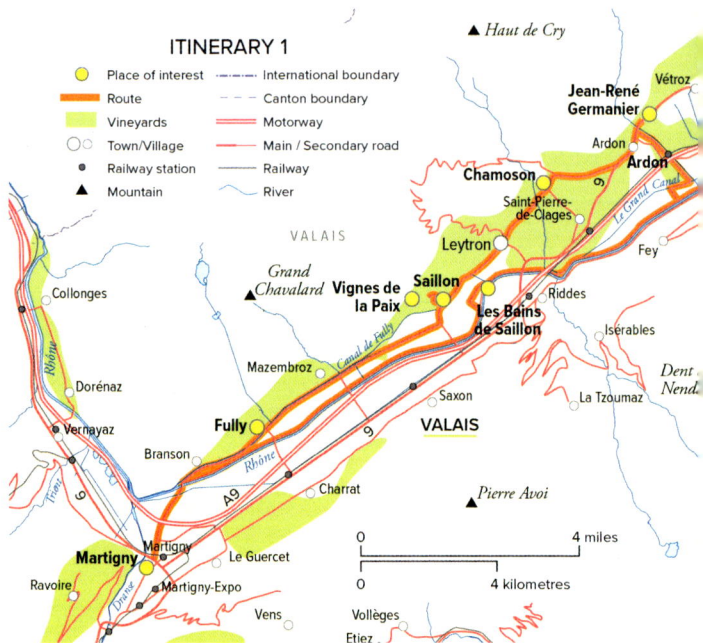

ITINERARY 1

🟡 Place of interest	·—··— International boundary
▬ Route	– – – Canton boundary
Vineyards	▬ Motorway
◯ ◌ Town/Village	▬ Main / Secondary road
• Railway station	▬ Railway
▲ Mountain	～ River

famed for its Petite Arvine. Stop at the **Maison de la Petite Arvine** (see p135) or pre-book tastings with Mathilde Roux at **Cave d'Orlaya**, Marie-Thérèse Chappaz at **Domaine Chappaz** (see p67) or Etienne and Raoul at **Cave Taramarcaz**.

Continue through Saxon to **Saillon**, one of Switzerland's oldest continuously inhabited villages and the birthplace of Joseph-Samuel Farinet – Valais' own Robin Hood. If you prefer to begin here, e-bikes can also be rented from the nearby **Relais de la Sarvaz** campsite. A handful of producers offer tasting experiences nearby, including **Cave Corbassière** and the Summer Bar at **Luisier Vin** (open Thursday-Saturday).

From the main road, a steep climb leads through Saillon's medieval ramparts into its old town. There is a clutch of restaurants here. Follow the cobblestone streets past **Tour Bayart** and into the upper vineyards, where stained-glass

panels depict episodes from Farinet's life.

Taking a small road to the left, you'll soon arrive at the **Vignes de la Paix** ('Vines of Peace') – leave your bikes at the entrance. This sacred plot is home to the world's smallest registered vineyard, now under the symbolic stewardship of the Dalai Lama. Around the site, plaques mark the visits of notable figures such as Ben Kingsley and Michael Schumacher. Take a moment here and enjoy the views across the Rhône Valley and its dramatic peaks.

Back on the bike, follow the vineyard road east for about 30 minutes toward **Leytron** and **Chamoson**. This stretch winds through rolling vineyards – busy at harvest time. Tasting options include **Cave Petite Vertu** and a guided vineyard experience with Scotsman Jamie McCulloch (see p122). For food, there's **OH!Berge** and **Restaurant Chez Madame**, both located on the main street.

Next comes a thrilling descent along the **Route du Vin** toward **Vétroz**, where Amigne is the star grape (see p56). At the roundabout, take a left and you'll soon arrive at the estate of **Jean-René Germanier** (see p121). Enjoy a guided tasting or a long lunch at their on-site restaurant.

From here, head down Avenue de la Gare and pass beneath the railway tracks at Ardon station. Within minutes you'll meet the **Rhône river path**. Turn left for a 30-minute ride to **Sion** – drop your bikes at the station and visit the twin hilltop castles (see p97) or ride further and enjoy a drink at **Celliers de Sion** (see p122). Turn right to follow the river's journey westward. After 30 minutes, detour to the **Bains de Saillon** for a soak in the thermal pools and a relaxed meal. The final leg traces the river past **Branson**, looping back into **Martigny** in around 45 minutes. Bring cash, make sure your bike is charged – and leave room for at least one bottle.

For more experiences in the region see pp135–136.

Vaud: Lavaux and Chablais
(Lausanne to Aigle)

Mode Train **Train time** (one way) 40
minutes **Distance** 44km (27 miles)

Take one of the most magical train rides
in the world: soon after leaving Lausanne,
when the track descends to the lakeshore,
it's as if the train is riding on the water
itself. From the other window, the Lavaux
vineyards rise steeply, reaching to the sky.

Lausanne is the perfect base for visiting
the Vaud region. The old town sits high
above Lake Geneva, while *Belle Epoque* lake
steamers leave from the charming port of
Ouchy down below. Use the modern metro
to get up and down the hills. The **Lausanne
Palace** (see p148) is a fine hotel in the centre,
while the **Beau-Rivage Palace** (see p148) offers luxury
lakeside comfort. The whole area is a gastronomic hub with
countless good food and wine options, including **La Table**
(see p162), the **Restaurant l'Hôtel de Ville** in **Crissier** (see
p164), **L'Appart** (see p173) and **Le Vieux-Lausanne**. A short
train ride takes you to the **Auberge de la Gare** in **Grandvaux**
(see p173). For great wine bars try **Street Cellar** and **Ta Cave**.

The many sights include **Notre-Dame** (a Gothic cathedral
with 13th-century stained-glass windows), **Plateforme
10** (a brand new arts district by the main station) and the
Olympic Museum by the lakeside promenade in Ouchy.
Take a stopping train to **Lutry**, only six minutes away from
Lausanne. Visit the **Terres de Lavaux** wine cooperative
just below Lutry station; for other wineries nearby see p31.
Alternatively, jump on the **Lavaux Express** tourist train (see
p137), leaving from the pier, for an effortless 1.25-hour road
trip through the vineyards.

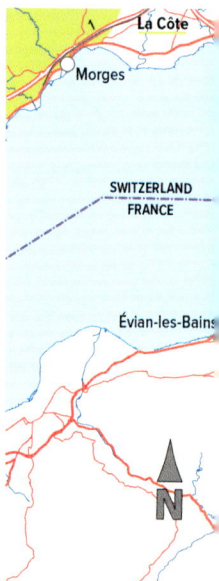

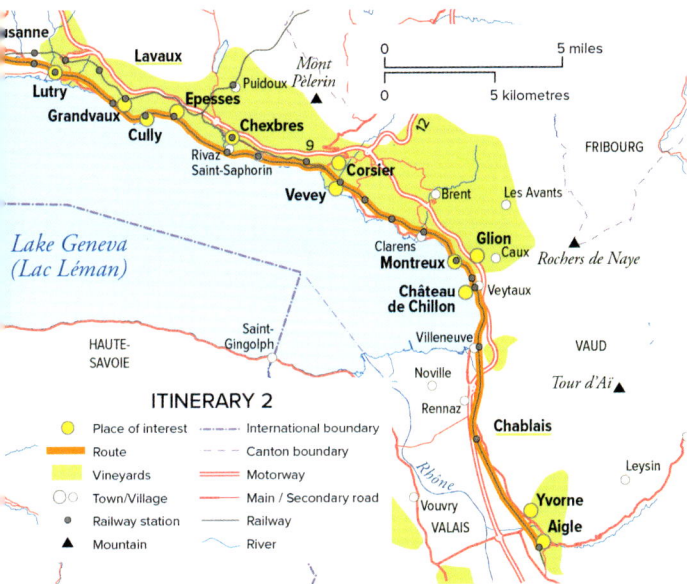

Map labels:

...sanne
Lavaux
Lutry
Grandvaux
Cully
Epesses
Chexbres
Mont Pèlerin ▲
Puidoux
9
Rivaz
Saint-Saphorin
Corsier
Vevey
Brent
Les Avants
FRIBOURG

Lake Geneva
(Lac Léman)

Clarens
Glion
Caux
Montreux
Rochers de Naye ▲
Château de Chillon
Veytaux

Saint-Gingolph
Villeneuve
VAUD

HAUTE-SAVOIE
Noville
Tour d'Aï ▲

Rennaz

ITINERARY 2

Chablais
Leysin

Rhône
Vouvry
VALAIS
Yvorne
Aigle

0 — 5 miles
0 — 5 kilometres

Legend:

- 🟡 Place of interest
- ▬ Route
- 🟨 Vineyards
- ◯◯ Town/Village
- ● Railway station
- ▲ Mountain
- ┈┈ International boundary
- ─── Canton boundary
- ─── Motorway
- ─── Main / Secondary road
- ─── Railway
- ─── River

Back on the train at Lutry, you reach the next village of **Cully** in less than five minutes. Lavaux Express also departs from nearby Cully pier and takes a different 1.25-hour route to the previous Lutry circuit.

Epesses, merely two minutes away by train from Cully, lies at the very heart of Lavaux. A 10-minute walk leads you to **Domaine Blaise Duboux** (see p124), where you will receive a perfect introduction to Chasselas and the Grand Cru wines of Dézaley and Calamin.

Take the stopping train towards Bex and, after 10 minutes, get off in **Vevey**. There are many great food options such as **Emotions par Guy Ravet** (see p158) at the **Grand Hôtel du Lac** and **Ze Fork** (see p174). If you fancy fondue or raclette, **Les Trois Sifflets** (see p174) is the perfect spot. **Le Poisson Rouge** (see p187) is a great wine bar in the old town with wines and atmosphere to match. Take time to stroll on the lakeside promenade that looks towards the Alps. The **Alimentarium** food museum (opposite the giant fork in the lake) merits a stop (10-min walk) and all cinephiles should head to **Chaplin's World** in Corsier (10-min bus) to learn about the life and times of Charlie Chaplin on the country estate where he retired.

The **Lavaux Panoramic** tourist train (see p137) runs different routes and tours from **Vevey** (main boat jetty) and also from **Chexbres** (10-min train ride from Vevey). In Chexbres, visit **Domaine Bovy** (see p125) for delicious Chasselas and one of the original wine tourism experiences in the region. Stay overnight at **Le Baron Tavernier Hotel & Spa** (see p149), less than 10 minutes walk, or at least sip a glass of Lavaux wine on **Le Deck** with its picture-postcard view.

From Vevey take the train to **Montreux**, the 'Pearl of Lake Geneva', less than 10 minutes away. Walk down to the lakeside where the promenade takes you past a statue of Freddie Mercury, who fell in love with the place. The musical highlight is the annual **Jazz Festival** in July. For a panoramic view of the Swiss and French Alps head up to the **Rochers de Naye** (50 min by cog railway from the main station). Visit the historic **Château de Chillon** (15 min by bus) set on a rock island in the lake. In **Glion** (15 min by train and funicular above Montreux), **Maison Décotterd** (see p163) serves fine cuisine and wine. In Montreux, eat and stay at **La Rouvenaz** near the lake or the **Hôtel de Rougemont & Spa** (see p149) up in the heart of the Vaud Alps (1.5 hr by panoramic MOB train from Montreux).

For the final leg go by train from Montreux to **Aigle**, barely 15 minutes away, in the Chablais subregion at the foot of the Swiss Alps. Visit the **Vine, Wine and Wine Label Museum** in the 12th-century **Château d'Aigle** (a 20-min walk – see p137) set amidst the vineyards. From the station take a bus to **Yvorne** (10 min) where you can walk in Winston Churchill's footsteps at the **Domaine de la Pierre Latine** and taste their Crosex Grillé Chasselas (see p69). Also book a visit to the **Artisans Vignerons d'Yvorne** (see p123), the regional cooperative. The fast train back returns you to **Lausanne** in 40 minutes.

For more experiences in the region see pp136–139.

Three exceptional wine trails invite you to discover and support Vaud's rich vineyard heritage

The **Route des Grands Crus de Lavaux** winds 2.8km (1.75 miles) through Dézaley and Calamin, the only Grands Cru appellations in Vaud. Eight information panels along the UNESCO-listed terraces reveal the secrets of these legendary vineyards. Accessible from Chexbres, Puidoux and Cully train stations, the route is free to explore and clearly signposted. Turn your stroll into meaningful support for the region's viticulture by scanning QR codes to buy from nearly 400 local producers at **vaudvins.ch**.

In the Chablais subregion, the **Sentier des Vignes** stretches 30km from Yvorne to Saint-Maurice, offering an immersive journey from Lake Geneva to the Alpine foothills. Nineteen dedicated signs share stories of the vines, while there are stops for tastings in historic cellars in places like Aigle and Bex. With its gentle elevation and easy access by public transport, this trail is perfect for exploring in stages while savouring the local wines and cuisine.

The **Balade des Capites** offers a more intimate experience, leading you through picturesque vineyards around the charming village of Féchy in La Côte. This accessible 4.5 km (2.8 mile) route takes about 2 hours and is marked by traditional *capites* (see p32) featuring info panels and interactive games. Along the way, visitors can enjoy self-service tastings and purchase wines on-site, making it a playful yet authentic encounter with the area's storied terroir.

Together, these three trails reveal Vaud's varied wine landscapes, combining outdoor adventure with unforgettable discoveries.

Route des Grands Crus de Lavaux

Sentier des Vignes

Balade des Capites

Content supported by the Office des Vins Vaudois

Vaud: Lavaux (Bossière to Cully)

Mode Walk/hike **Time** 2 hours (excluding stops)
Distance 7km (4.3 miles) **Elevation gain** 100m
(320ft)

A gentle meander with exceptional views, this scenic hike takes you through Lavaux's iconic terraces – and there are numerous wine stops along the way. Starting high above the lake in the hamlet of **Bossière**, the trail winds east through some of the region's most photogenic sites.

Best reached by train, there are direct hourly departures from **Lausanne** (8 min) or **Montreux/Vevey** (45 min) to Bossière, all year round. From the station platform closest to the lake, head east along the marked trail. Within minutes, you'll be walking next to the vines of Lutry – Chasselas left, right and centre – with dramatic lake and mountain views. The path is mostly flat, with a few short ascents and clear signage throughout.

After around 30 minutes, you'll reach the **Pont Bory** viaduct and a prime photo stop. With luck, you'll see one of the paddle steamers plying between Lausanne and Evian in France. Not long after, you can descend to **Domaine du Daley** for a tasting or continue for 10 minutes to **Domaine Piccard**, known for its low-intervention, unfiltered wines. Look out for the 'honour wine fridge' on the vineyard path, just above the panoramic **Domaine Vitis Musicalis** (see p126); chilled bottles and cups available, cash only. A few minutes on, you'll spot Viticalis' two *capites* – stone vineyard huts, perfect for a pause en route. The narrow trail then hugs the railway line, winding through a wooded patch before unveiling the amphitheatre-like slopes and terraces of **Villette**.

Ten minutes further on you'll reach upper **Grandvaux**. Visit **Domaine Croix Duplex**, or enjoy lunch at the nearby

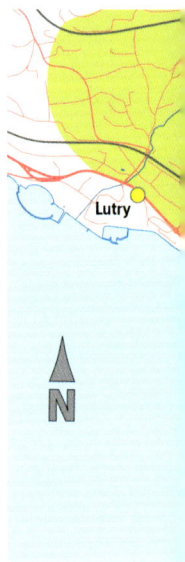

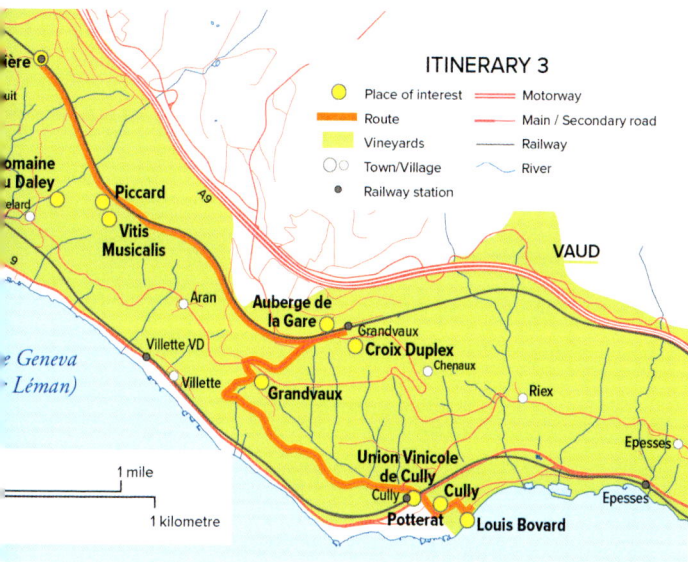

ITINERARY 3

○	Place of interest	══	Motorway
▬	Route	──	Main / Secondary road
▨	Vineyards	──	Railway
○○	Town/Village	～	River
●	Railway station		

Auberge de la Gare (see p173). Alternatively, follow the pedestrian signs for 15 minutes down into the heart of the old village – a former Roman settlement. Spend 30 minutes wandering the storied cobbled streets, the old Latin Quarter and **Maison Maillardo's** 16th-century late-gothic windows.

There's also plenty to sip: **Domaine Joly**, **Cave du Vieux Pressoir** and **Caveau Corto** (open weekend evenings) offer tastings with prior reservation. For food and wine pairings, stop at **Tout un Monde** restaurant (located in a former church) or nearby **Domaine de la Crausaz** (see p186) and its uninterrupted terrace views.

Continue downhill for about 20 minutes to the village of **Cully** for a lakeside finale. There are more tasting options at **Louis Bovard**, **Potterat** and **Union Vinicole** (UVC) for wine and artisan chocolate. Cully station serves direct trains to Lausanne and Montreux. Or alternatively take the seasonal ferry from Cully port for a totally scenic send-off.

For more experiences in the region see pp136–137.

Geneva: Between Arve and Lake (Corsinge to Cologny via Jussy)

Mode Walk/hike & bus **Time** 3.5 hours (excluding stops) **Distance** (walking) 15km (9 miles) **Elevation gain** 100m (320ft)

Winding through forest paths and vineyard-covered hills, this scenic walk offers a slower, more flavourful way to explore Geneva's countryside. Along the route, expect intimate cellar tastings, protected wildlife... and wide mountain vistas.

Make **Geneva** your base and take an easy bus ride to **Corsinge**. From here, pick up the official **'Entre Arve et Lac' Trail** (Route 105), following signposts through undulating countryside and peaceful hamlets. This gentle section of the route meanders past orchards, forest edges and fields, with views stretching towards **Mont Salève** on one side, Lake Geneva and Jura peaks on the other. Along the way, keep an eye out for the information panels that describe Geneva's grape varieties and winemaking techniques.

Arriving in Jussy, you have two tasting options. Pause at the gardens of **La Gara** (see p127), where Adeline Wegmüller produces her small collection of biodynamic wines. Alternatively, visit the grand **Domaine Château du Crest**, one of the canton's best-known estates. For lunch, book ahead at **Auberge de la Couronne** for refined seasonal fare or grab a seat at the relaxed **Chez Martine**.

Just before reaching **Choulex**, the path passes the **Marais du Château** – a protected wetland nature reserve with open fields, wild grasses and birdlife. This is also horse

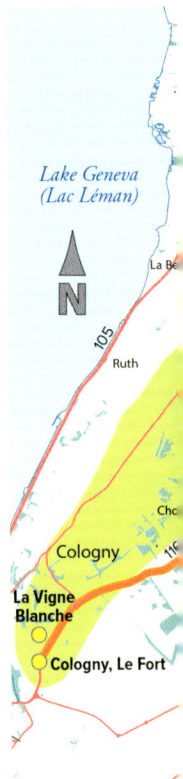

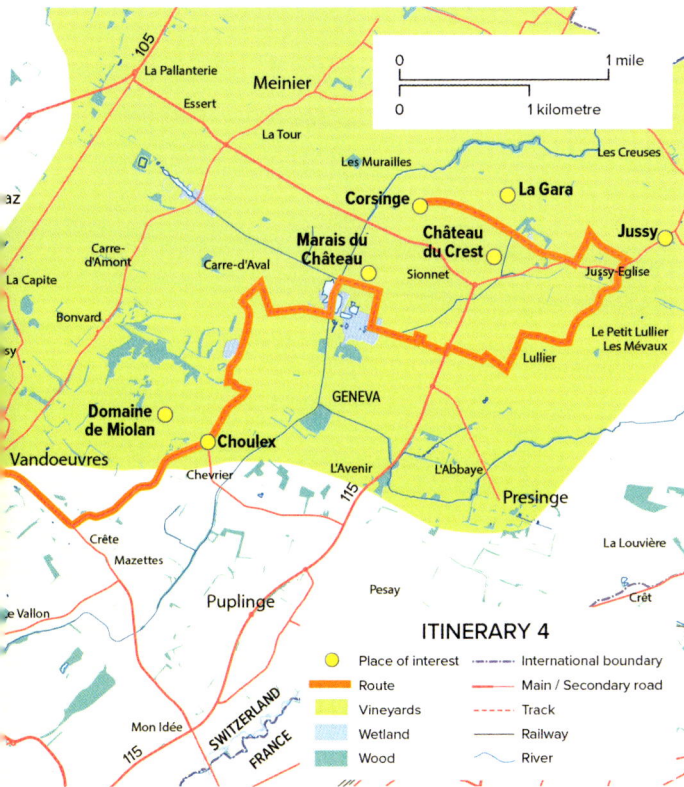

ITINERARY 4

Legend:
- ● Place of interest
- ▬ Route
- Vineyards
- Wetland
- Wood
- ┄ International boundary
- ─ Main / Secondary road
- ┄ Track
- ─ Railway
- River

country, due to the many riding schools in the area. With a reservation, stop at **Domaine de Miolan**, where Bertrand Favre crafts his terroir-driven wines.

From Choulex, hop on Bus 33 (every 30 min) to reach **Cologny**, where a final visit to **Domaine de la Vigne Blanche** (see p126) and winemaker Sarah Favre rounds off the day away from the bustle of Geneva city.

From here it's an easy 30-minute walk to **Geneva** or take Bus A from Cologny, Le Fort.

For more experiences in the region see p139.

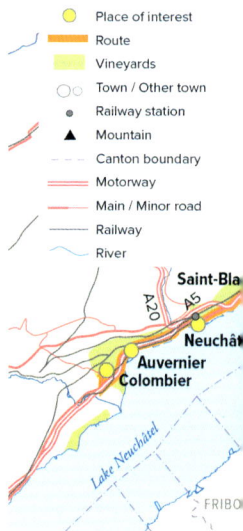

Three Lakes: Biel/Bienne, Neuchâtel, Morat/Murten

Mode Car **Driving time** 2.5 hours
Distance 148km (92 miles)

The Jura mountains, not the Alps, form the backdrop to this route, which follows the shores of the three lakes that define the region. The roads criss-cross the invisible *Röstigraben* (see p35) and let you experience French and German languages, cultures and foods.

Discover Switzerland's capital by making **Bern** your base. The old town is a UNESCO World Heritage site and its **medieval arcades**, **cathedral** and **Zytglogge** (clocktower) are an easy walk. Visits to the **Bern bear park** and the **Einstein Museum** are well worth it. For a creative culinary experience, book a table at **Restaurant MYLE** (see p179) near the station. The **Hotel Schweizerhof and Spa** or the **Hotel Bären am Bundesplatz** are good overnight options in the city centre.

On your way to wine country, stop en route in **Biel/Bienne** (just 40 mins away on the A6 motorway), the world's watchmaking capital. Visit the **Swatch** and **Omega** museums at the **Cité du Temps** (City of Time). Check out the historic fountains in the old town and pop into the wine bar **Ici C'est Le Vin** for a first taste of the local wines.

Head on Route 5 to **Schott Weine** (see p129) in **Twann** on Lake Biel/Bienne, less than 20 minutes from Biel. Stay on Route 5 for another 15 minutes and cross the *Röstigraben* into canton Neuchâtel. Stop at **Grillette Domaine de Cressier** (see p40) to see how the estate follows the lunar calendar. Head towards **Neuchâtel** for 10 more minutes and

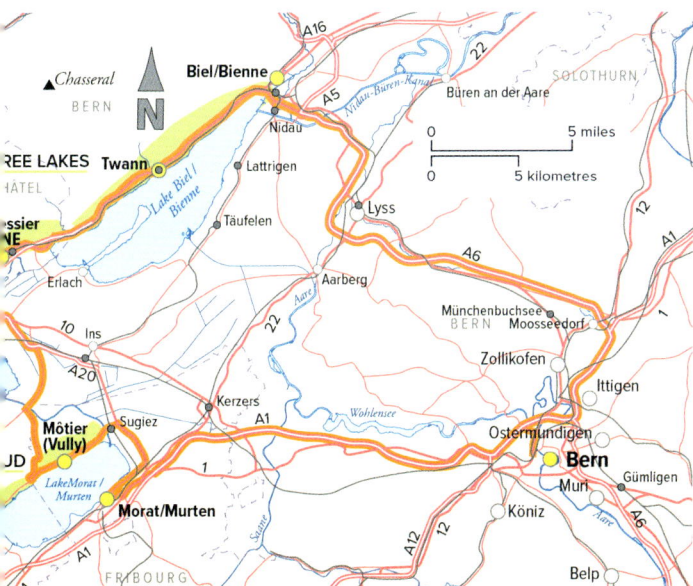

visit **Domaine Saint-Sébaste** in **St Blaise** for great *Oeil de Perdrix* rosé (see p61).

Neuchâtel is 15 minutes further along Lake Neuchâtel. Walk in the old town and take in the panoramic views at the 1,000-year-old **Château de Neuchâtel** (literally, 'Castle of Newcastle'). Sample the local AOC wines at **Oenothèque Chauffage Compris** wine bar (see p189) and eat at **Brasserie le Jura** (see p186), both just five minutes' walk from the castle. If you make it a two-day trip, take a leisurely boat trip on the lake for the best view of the vineyards and spend a night at the remarkable **Hôtel Palafitte** (see p151) on the lake.

Ten minutes further on is **Auvernier**, where wine has been made for over 400 years at the **Château d'Auvernier** (see p128). Allow time to visit **Domaine de la Maison Carrée** and **Domaine Bouvet-Jabloir**, both around the corner. A good meal stop here is the **Brasserie du Poisson** (see p175). Before heading to the next lake, sample fine Pinot Noir at **Domaine de Chambleau** in **Colombier**, perched just above Auvernier.

Turn back on Route 5 towards Biel and, after 15 minutes, follow signs to **Mont-Vully** and **Môtier** for another 15 minutes. Visit **Le Petit Château** (see p128) and **Cru de l'Hôpital**, where Christian Vessaz is known for outstanding biodynamic wines. Learn more about the area's history on the **Vully Vineyard Walk** (see p140). A short detour to the picturesque old town of **Morat (Murten)** with its 12 fortress towers is highly recommended. You can be back in **Bern** within 30 minutes via the A1 motorway.

For more experiences in the region see pp139–140.

ITINERARY 6

German-speaking Region: Zürich, Schaffhausen & Winterthur

Mode Train **Train time** 2 hours **Distance** 101km (63 miles)

This route guides you through two of the most important subregions of the German-speaking Region: Zürich and Schaffhausen. The regular trains from Zürich stop frequently and allow you to visit the smaller towns and villages along the route.

Zürich, Switzerland's largest city, is the ideal base and offers a wide choice of restaurants: **KLE** (see p166), **Blaue Ente** (see p178), **Zunfthaus zur Waage** and **Frau Gerolds Garten** as well as wine bars: **Widder Bar** (see p191) and **Chez Smith** (see p189). Splendid hotel options include The **Dolder Grand** (see p156) and **Park Hyatt Zurich** (see p156).

Walk in the old town with its landmark churches – **Peterskirche**, **Fraumünster** and **Grossmünster**. Football fans should head to the **FIFA museum** (10 min by tram) and chocoholics to the **Lindt Home of Chocolate** in Kilchberg (25 min by train). To visit a Lake Zürich winery, head south to **JET**

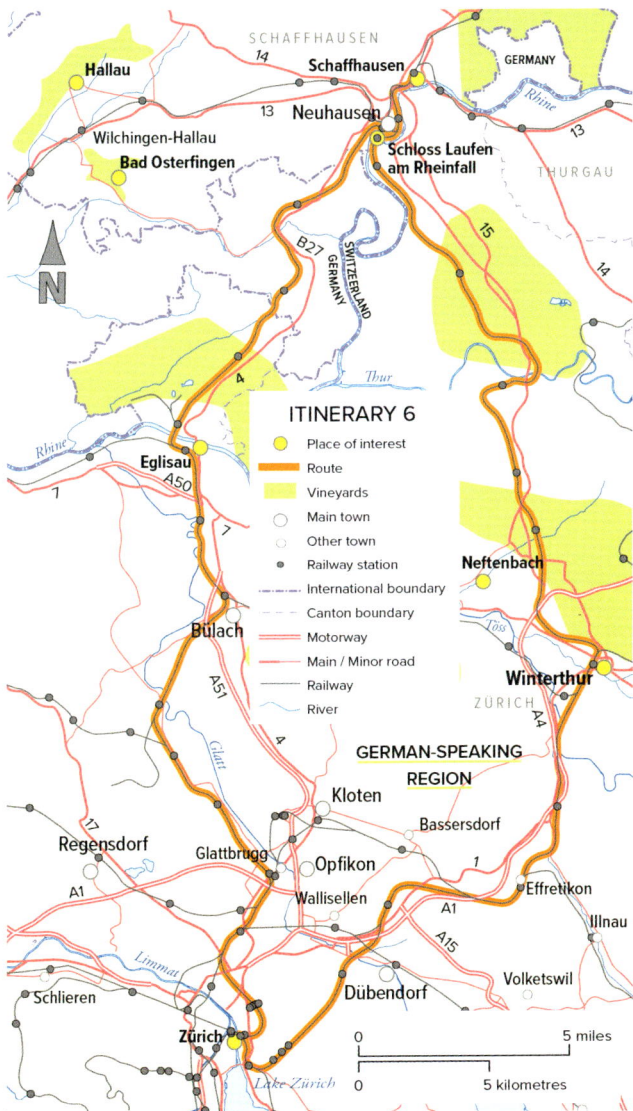

SCHAFFHAUSEN

Hallau

GERMANY

Schaffhausen

Neuhausen

13

14

Wilchingen-Hallau

Bad Osterfingen

Schloss Laufen
am Rheinfall

THURGAU

Rhine

13

15

14

B27

SWITZERLAND
GERMANY

Thur

4

Rhine

Eglisau

A50

7

7

7

Neftenbach

Töss

Bülach

A51

Winterthur

ZÜRICH

A4

4

GERMAN-SPEAKING
REGION

Glatt

Kloten

Bassersdorf

Regensdorf

17

Glattbrugg

Opfikon

Effretikon

A1

Wallisellen

1

A1

Illnau

A15

Limmat

Volketswil

Schlieren

Dübendorf

Zürich

Lake Zürich

ITINERARY 6

- ● Place of interest
- ▬ Route
- Vineyards
- ○ Main town
- ○ Other town
- ● Railway station
- –·–· International boundary
- – – – Canton boundary
- ——— Motorway
- ——— Main / Minor road
- ——— Railway
- ——— River

0	5 miles

0	5 kilometres

Wein (see p130) in **Uetikon am See** (45-min train and walk).

Before you jump on a train from Zürich, pop into **Baur au Lac Vins** (see p197), the fine wine shop at the main station.

110 Take the stopping train north towards Schaffhausen and, after half an hour, get off at **Eglisau** to visit two wineries overlooking the Rhine: **Bechtel Weine** (15-min walk) and **Weingut Pircher** (35-min walk) produce some of the top AOC Zürich wines.

Continue by train to **Schaffhausen**. Walk in the old town with its 400-year-old **Munot Fortress** and visit the **Museum zu Allerheiligen**, an old Benedictine monastery. One of Schaffhausen's top wineries is **aagne weingut** (see p129) in **Hallau**. Take the train to **Wilchingen-Hallau** then a short walk (20 min) to get there or, in summer, book a horse-drawn carriage tour (see p141) from the station. While in Hallau pop into the **Weinkrone Museum** (see p142) in a former winegrower's house to see how wine used to be made.

The winery at **Bad Osterfingen** has a good restaurant (see p178) and comfortable guest house (see p152) just a 20-minute bus ride and walk from Wilchingen-Hallau station.

Back in Schaffhausen, take the train south towards Winterthur. After five minutes get off at **Schloss Laufen am Rheinfall**. The castle stands right above the thundering **Rhine Falls** and is also a good place to take a two-hour **Ship & Wine** cruise on the Rhine (see p142).

Continue by train to **Winterthur**, a perfect stop for museum lovers – modern art at the **Kunstmuseum**, impressionism at **'am Römerholz'**, Swiss, German and Austrian art at the **Reinhart am Stadtgartenmuseum** and contemporary photography at the **Fotomuseum Winterthur**. Children will love the interactive displays at **The Swiss Science Center Technorama** (15 min by train and bus).

Neftenbach (30-min bus and walk) is home to **Weingut Nadine Saxer**, one of Zürich's most celebrated producers with some of the region's finest white wines. Return to Winterthur, where a fast train will return you to **Zürich** in 20 minutes.

For more experiences in the region see pp141–143.

German-speaking Region: Bündner Herrschaft (Graubünden)

Mode e-bike **Cycling time** 1.5 hours **Distance** 25km (15.5 miles) **Elevation gain** 225m (740ft)

This idyllic subregion of Graubünden sits between Liechtenstein to the north, Europe's fourth-smallest country, and Chur to the south, one of the oldest settlements in Switzerland. It's small enough to discover comfortably by bicycle and an e-bike makes the journey even more leisurely. The roads connecting the wine villages are not very busy and the wineries and other places to stop are close to one another.

Bad Ragaz is the perfect base for exploring this area.

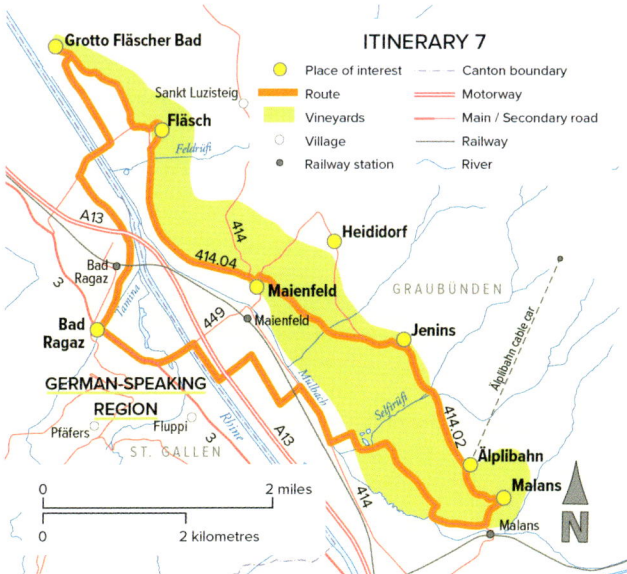

ITINERARY 7

- ⬤ Place of interest
- ▬ Route
- ▨ Vineyards
- ○ Village
- ⬤ Railway station
- – – – Canton boundary
- ▬ Motorway
- ▬ Main / Secondary road
- ▬ Railway
- ∿ River

Grotto Fläscher Bad
Sankt Luzisteig
Fläsch
Feldrüti
A13
Bad Ragaz
Bad Ragaz
GERMAN-SPEAKING REGION
Pfäfers
Flüppi
ST. GALLEN
414
414.04
Maienfeld
Maienfeld
449
Heididorf
GRAUBÜNDEN
Jenins
Älplibahn cable car
414.02
Älplibahn
Malans
Malans
N

You can rent your e-bike next to the **Tamina Therme** (ebikestation.ch) from May to October, then soothe your muscles in the thermal baths after your ride or stay overnight at the **Grand Resort Bad Ragaz**, which offers a choice of hotels and a range of wellness facilities.

Less than a mile (1.6km) from the start you cross the Rhine and, after several turnings, reach the vineyards. The first 4.8km (3 miles) are on the level. Then the road climbs gently for the next 5.6km (3.5 miles) between the vineyards via **Malans**. Just let the e-bike take the strain. On the way to Malans, head to the new winery at **Weingut Fromm** (see p131). In the village itself, visit **Domaine Donatsch** (see p130) with its family tavern **'zum Ochsen'** next door and also stop at **Wegelin Weine**, known for its Pinot Noir and increasingly for its whites.

As you leave Malans, take a short detour to the **Älplibahn** (May to November) where you can leave your bike and take a small cable-car up to a high mountain ridge. You will be greeted by great views of the Rhine Valley below and a mountain restaurant serving tasty local dishes.

Carry on for another mile and a half (2.4km) to **Jenins**, the highest point of the route – vineyards on the left, woods on the right. This village is home to **Weingut Obrecht** as well as **Annatina Pelizzatti Weinbau**, who runs the estate with her daughter, Laura, and only sells her wines in Switzerland. The **Alter Torkel** (see pp43 and 140) on the far side of Jenins is a good restaurant option in a beautiful vineyard setting. If the first half of the ride has exhausted you, spend a night inside a converted wine barrel at the **Schlaf-Fass** (see p156).

The road drops down to **Maienfeld** where the **Schloss Maienfeld** restaurant (see p180) and **Stall 247** wine bar (see p190) are welcoming places to recharge. The nearby **Möhr-Niggli Weingut** is committed to sustainable viticulture and produces fine reds and whites. A short detour leads you up to **Heididorf**, where a 19th-century Alpine village has been recreated in celebration of the famous literary character Heidi (see p44).

Leave Jenins on the Fläscherstrasse, the left fork heading

north-west to **Fläsch**. On your right, just before you reach the village, ride past the modern **Weingut Gantenbein** (not open for visits). Visit **Weingut Hermann** at the far end of Fläsch and then stop at the winery's grotto restaurant; it's just a short ride outside the village and serves a range of his older vintages.

The 4.8km (3 mile) ride back to **Bad Ragaz** takes about 20 minutes. There you can enjoy even more of the local wines with a memorable meal at either the **Restaurant Rössli** or **IGNIV** at the Grand Resort (see p166).

For more experiences in the region see pp141–143.

ITINERARY 8

Ticino: Sottoceneri (Mendrisio/Lake Lugano)

Mode Car **Driving time** 2.25 hours **Distance** 85km (53 miles)

The awesome lake and mountain views of the Sottoceneri make it hard to keep your eyes on the road. Just remind yourself that you do want to visit a few wineries before sunset. Take your pick, as this route includes more than you can cover in a single day.

Lugano is the best operating base for Ticino and the **Villa Castagnola** (see p158) is the ideal place to stay. Make time to stroll around the **Piazza della Riforma** and the arcades on **Via Nassa**, as well as the spacious **Parco Ciani** down by the lake. Savour fine Mediterranean cuisine and the best of the region's wines at **Badalucci** (see p181). The surrounding mountains offer spectacular outlooks and are easily accessible: the funicular to **Monte Brè** (to the east) is very close to Villa Castagnola and the funicular to **San Salvatore** (to the south) leaves from **Paradiso** (a 15-min drive).

The first stop is around **Mendrisio**, an area rich in vineyards at Switzerland's southern tip next to Italy. You can cover most of the 24km (15 miles) there in under half

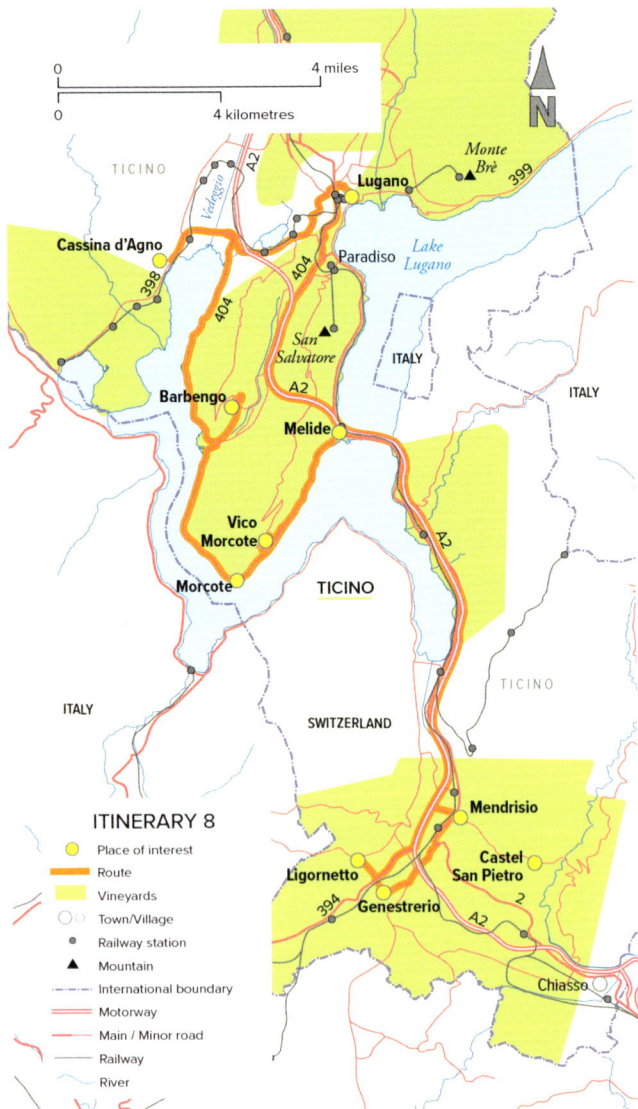

0   4 miles

0   4 kilometres

N

TICINO

Vedeggio

Lugano

Monte Brè
▲ 399

Cassina d'Agno

398

404

404

Paradiso

Lake Lugano

San Salvatore ▲

ITALY

ITALY

A2

Barbengo

Melide

Vico Morcote

Morcote

TICINO

A2

ITALY

SWITZERLAND

TICINO

Mendrisio

ITINERARY 8

- ⬤ Place of interest
- ▬ Route
- ▮ Vineyards
- ◯◯ Town/Village
- ⬤ Railway station
- ▲ Mountain
- ⋯ International boundary
- — Motorway
- — Main / Minor road
- ┈ Railway
- ～ River

Ligornetto

Castel San Pietro

394

Genestrerio

A2

2

Chiasso

an hour via the A2 motorway. Start at **Vinattieri** (see p133) in **Ligornetto** and then continue to **Agriloro**, just 3.2km (2 miles) away in **Genestrerio**. In Mendrisio itself, less than 10 minutes to the north, **Fa'Wino** (see p133) and **Gialdi** (see p182) are small and large-scale wineries respectively. Shopaholics be warned: the vast **FoxTown Factory Stores** are right here – 160 stores, 250 international brands and big discounts. In case you require some sustenance by this point, the **Osteria Cuntitt** is only 10 minutes away in **Castel San Pietro**.

Head back north on the motorway and exit just before the causeway across **Lake Lugano**. Follow signs to **Swissminiatur** in **Melide**, where 128 authentic scaled models of Switzerland's major landmarks are displayed in an open-air exhibit, including model railways, lake steamers, cable cars and more – equally great fun for adults and children.

Take the lake road south to reach **Tenuta Castello di Morcote** (see p158) in **Vico Morcote**, which sits on a peninsula with glorious views. A good option for food is **La Sorgente** restaurant at the nearby **Relais Castello di Morcote**. For an extended trip, it also makes a great overnight stop. Carry on round the peninsula for 15 minutes to **Morcote** and visit **Parco Scherrer** (March to October), a lush subtropical park on the lakeside. For more outdoor excitement, jump on one of the most beautiful swings in the world in the village centre.

Follow the lake road northwards and, after 10 minutes, turn off towards **Cantina Kopp von der Krone Visini** in **Barbengo**. This modern winery produces fine Merlot-based wines and a wide range of whites, sparkling and grappa. Return to the lake road and head 11.3km (7 miles) further north to reach **Tenuta San Giorgio**, hidden away in **Cassina d'Agno** – a sustainability pioneer producing innovative special editions. On the way back to **Lugano**, **Fattoria Moncucchetto** (see p132) is well worth a stop, not only for its winery but also its on-site restaurant.

For more experiences in the region see p143.

Grape Escapes: spectacular overnight stays with views of Swiss vineyards

Unique accommodation in the heart of the Swiss vineyards – that's Grape Escapes, where you can discover Switzerland as a wine country and stay in extraordinary places that are as diverse and charming as the wines themselves.

Whether you sleep in an old wine barrel, under the stars or on the water, **Grape Escapes** offers unforgettable nights in or near the picturesque Swiss vineyards. The project is a collaboration between Switzerland Tourism and Swiss Wine and combines the best of the local wine culture with creative accommodation.

Six wine regions, over 60 experiences

There are currently more than 60 accommodations to choose from, spread across the six wine-growing regions of Switzerland. Each area has its unique landscape and cultural identity – from Alpine valleys and Mediterranean-style hills to idyllic lake landscapes. **Grape Escapes** allows wine lovers to plan their own personal journey of discovery through the diversity of Switzerland's wine regions.

These accommodations are not only stylish retreats, but also opportunities to experience Switzerland's wine country up close: whether gazing out of the window at the vines, strolling through the

Attila Boutique Boatel, Lake Neuchâtel

Birdbox Curzútt, Ticino

La Capite, Domaine de Calamin, Epesses, Vaud

vineyards or enjoying a glass of wine right where it was made.

Experience Swiss wine with all your senses

Rustic or modern, cozy or unusual, each accommodation embodies authenticity, regionality and a culture of enjoyment. The basic idea is that those who love Swiss wine don't just want to taste it, they want to experience how and where it is produced.

Many hosts also offer wine cellar tours, tastings or discussions with winemakers. This gives guests even deeper insights into the traditional craft and philosophy of Swiss viticulture.

Highlights include a historic vineyard cottage in Vaud, a modern cube with panoramic windows in Ticino, a bubble hotel in Thurgau with unobstructed views of the stars and a cargo e-bike with an integrated tent for mobile wine adventures in Schaffhausen.

Further information and booking options can be found at **switzerland.com/grape-escapes**

The Swiss Wine Gourmet label

For smart wine travellers looking for restaurants that serve Swiss wines, this online guide is just the thing. Over 1,300 restaurants already carry this award for offering a good to excellent selection of Swiss wines. Discover the Swiss Wine Gourmet restaurants in your area and find your new favourite local wine.

swisswinegourmet.ch

SWISS WINE GOURMET

Content supported by Swiss Wine Promotion

LISTINGS PREPARED BY

Marc Checkley
Simon Hardy
Nina Caplan
Simone Aïda Baur

The Guide

Contents

CLUB OENOLOGIQUE

The Guide is produced in partnership with Club Oenologique, the premium lifestyle publication connecting people to the joys of the world through the lens of wine and spirits

Scan for the latest on Switzerland, and expert guides to food and drink regions around the world

The best Swiss wineries for tours and tastings

A splash of Chasselas, a sunset barbecue, a long-table lunch in the vines... we list the Swiss wineries that welcome the wine-curious and the wine lover alike.

Domaine Jean-René Germanier

Wine tourism in Switzerland is having its moment. A growing number of wine estates now open their doors to curious wine lovers, offering tastings, cellar visits and the occasional long-table lunch overlooking ancient Alpine castles. But it's still yet to match the efficiency of the national rail system. Some places remain... elusive. These are small, often family-run operations, and welcoming guests isn't always the top priority. You might see 'open' online, knock on the cellar door and be met with nothing but a cat and a locked gate.

The trick? Plan ahead, make an appointment, learn a few pleasantries in the local language and lower your expectations – until the wine starts pouring. Swiss hospitality will kick in. Just not always on your schedule.

Whether it's a splash of Chasselas straight from the barrel or rosé at a winemaker's sunset barbecue, there's something to enjoy in every region. Vaud leads the pack with its experiences and expanding wine tourism network, but other regions are catching up fast – particularly Graubünden and Valais, where you can taste Provins's finest reserves in mountain caverns – or feast on a vintner's barbecue at JET Wein overlooking Lake Zürich. Here we list over 20 of the best wineries and estates open to visitors. For more ideas, see **The best Swiss wine tourism experiences** (p134).

Valais

Domaine Jean-René Germanier

Balavaud, Route Cantonale 291, 1963 Vétroz

Train station Sion

On the same site since 1896, Jean-René Germanier has evolved from its roots in orchard farming to become one of Switzerland's best-known wine producers. From Monday to Saturday the house runs regular tours and generous tastings in English, French and German. Highlights are visiting the 'starlight' barrel-room and the Cayas Library, dedicated to the estate's multi-awarded Syrah – born of Valais. There is also an on-site restaurant, serving excellent Valaisian delicacies. Active larger groups can take a guided tour to some of the domaine's highest vineyards – paired with raclette and wine. jrgermanier.ch

McCulloch Wines

Rue Plane-ville 22,
1955 Chamoson

Train station Riddes

A rarity in these parts, Scotsman
Jamie McCulloch moved to
Switzerland for love 25 years
ago. The love ended but he
remained smitten with all
things Swiss. Jamie put himself
through viticultural school and
soon after set up his own winery.
Producing approximately 30,000
bottles a year, he splits his
range between two labels: Les
Deux Cimes (traditional styles)
and his 'Magic' crafted series.
Tastings in English, French,
German – and Scots – are held
by appointment. He can also
organize e-bike and walking
tours with expert guides.

mcculloch-wines.com

Les Celliers de Sion

Route d'Italie 9, 1950 Sion

Train station Sion

A sight to behold, the winery's
eye-catching iridescent panels

McCulloch Wines

Les Celliers de Sion

reflect the sun's rays throughout
the day. Anchored at the
foot of the vertigo-inducing
Clavau vineyards, Les Celliers
is a collaboration between the
Varone and Bonvin wine families,
offering a host of tasting
experiences all year round. From
May to late October, a self-
guided vineyard walk leads to
the Bisse de Clavau (a medieval
irrigation system), culminating
in a lunch and tasting at the old
winemaker's hut, high above
the Rhône Valley. The bar is a
great location for exploring the
dozens of wines available. It's a
wine experience of theme park
proportions. Open 7 days a week
till 8pm (6pm on Sundays).
Lunch bookings essential.

celliers.ch

Provins

Rue de l'Industrie 22, 1950 Sion

Train station Sion

Provins is Switzerland's largest
winery, producing 6% of the
country's wine and boasting a
collection of over 100 styles.

Twice named Swiss Winery of the Year, it offers more than just tastings: from June to September, a guided day-tour takes you to the 285m (935ft) high Grande Dixence dam. Afterwards, venture into cavernous tunnels set deep within ancient Alpine rock, where the award-winning 'Titans' wines mature in massive barrels. A hearty lunch rounds out the journey. For a gentler experience, the new wine bar (closed Sundays) and Afterwork Tastings await at lower altitudes.

provins.ch

St Jodern Kellerei

Unterstalden 2,
3932 Visperterminen

Train station Visp

At around 1,150m (3,373ft), this

St Jodern Kellerei

cooperative has some of the highest vines in Switzerland. With close to two dozen styles, their Heida wines (see p60) garner much attention. The recently renovated cellar, open Monday to Saturday, offers a trio of tours and tasting experiences paired with Valaisian cured meats from a local butcher. As well as tasting the wines, you might get the chance to pick up some of the local Swiss-German dialect. Keep a keen eye out for the 'man in the mountain' during the cellar tour.

jodernkellerei.ch

Vaud

Artisans Vignerons d'Yvorne

Les Maisons Neuves 5,
1853 Yvorne

Train station Aigle

In the far eastern reaches of Vaud, the Artisans Vignerons d'Yvorne (AVY) have been shaping Chablais wines since 1902. This 120-member

Provins – Domaine Tourbillon, Sion

Artisans Vignerons d'Yvorne

cooperative cultivates 55ha (136 acres) across a jigsaw of ancient soils. The distinct terroir reveals itself in AVY's award-winning Chant des Resses, while Doral, Syrah and Pinot Noir (see pp61-65) reflect the breadth and depth of the region. Tastings run Monday to Saturday, with special group visits by appointment.

avy.ch

Blaise Duboux

Sentier de Creyvavers 3,
1098 Epesses

Train station Epesses

The storyteller of Lavaux, Blaise is the 17th generation of this small family estate, tucked away in the village of Epesses. A passionate adopter of both organic and biodynamic viticultural methods, he lives and breathes terroir, and is full of stories demonstrating its effect on the grapes and its uniqueness in Lavaux. A proactive member of the winemaking community, Blaise also helped found the Plant Robert Association, a group of more than a dozen winemakers charged with the protection of this rare Gamay-like grape variety (see p62). Open from 9am on Saturdays, or by appointment during the week.

blaiseduboux.ch

Blaise Duboux (right)

Domaine Bovy

Rue du Bourg de Plaît 15,
1071 Chexbres

Train station Chexbres

One of the first wineries to embrace wine tourism, the Bovys offer a range of tasting experiences complemented with expansive views across the vines of Dézaley. Regular cellar tours and tastings run all year round on weekdays and Saturday mornings, held in the glasshouse or on the panoramic terrace. From May to late September, they host Tapas Thursdays at sunset, regular barbecue events, and on Sundays an Electrobrunch with a live DJ. Bookings advised.

domainebovy.ch

Domaine de Penloup, Graenicher Wines

Chemin de Penloup 3,
1180 Tartegnin

Train station Rolle

Named after the legendary wolf that prowled the nearby woods more than 100 years ago, this small estate is perched on the upper slopes of La Côte. Vincent Graenicher and his Danish wife Astrid have spent the past decade developing terroir-specific, co-plantation and single parcel wines, also converting to organic. His dozen wines, including an audacious Merlot Réserve,

Domaine Bovy

represent a clear commitment to sustainable viticulture. The Nordic-inspired tasting room is open on Wednesday evenings and Saturday mornings; other times by appointment. Views of Mont Blanc are common – but not guaranteed.

graenicher-vins.ch

Domaine Henri Cruchon

Route du Village 32,
1112 Echichens

Train station Morges

Driven by passion and family legacy, Catherine Cruchon now leads the estate her grandfather

Domaine de Penloup

founded in 1976. Located in a hilltop village near Morges, the estate grows 16 grape varieties, all cultivated biodynamically across diverse plots, highlighting the character of La Côte. Catherine's expertise shines through both in the estate's classic wines and her own line of special cuvées. Tastings are intimate, with the family's story being front and centre. For a deeper dive, masterclasses can be organized to explore the wines in greater detail. Open daily; no appointment needed for regular tastings.

henricruchon.com

Domaine Vitis Musicalis
Chemin du Daley 119,
1095 Bourg-en-Lavaux

Train station Grandvaux

Musical by name, musical by nature, winemaker Alain Chollet's family has been

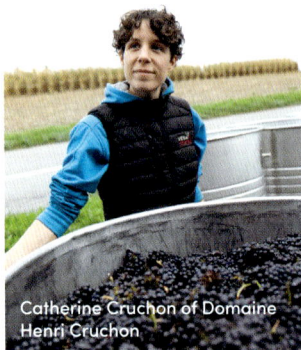
Catherine Cruchon of Domaine Henri Cruchon

in Lavaux for more than 200 years. Alain, the fourth generation winemaker, is a keen saxophonist and seduces his grapes with an eclectic mix of jazz and pop – on the vine and in the cellar. Tastings of his wines are by appointment on weekdays and are hosted by Alain himself or his son-in-law Stéphane. Alternatively, reserve a fondue dinner in their large windowed barrels set amongst the vines of Villette. In winter, the wines can be enjoyed in a transparent igloo with views of the lake from every angle.

vitismusicalis.ch

Geneva
Domaine de la Vigne Blanche
Route de Vandoeuvres 13, 1223 Cologny

Train station Geneva

More than a century ago, a lone white vine stood in the fields of Cologny. Where some saw an

Domaine Vitis Musicalis

Domaine de la Vigne Blanche

omen, the Meylan family saw opportunity. Today, winemaker Sarah Meylan-Favre carries on her grandfather's legacy, tending 7.5ha (18.5 acres) of organic-certified vineyards on slopes above Lake Geneva. On Friday evenings and Saturday mornings Sarah welcomes visitors to the old cellar to taste her dozen wines. Make sure to sample the rare *L'Esprit de Genève* – a red blend made by only seven local winemakers.

lavigneblanche.ch

La Gara

Route de la Gara 36, 1254 Jussy

Train station Chêne-Bourg

A 30-minute drive from the city, you'll find Geneva's secret garden. This enchanting estate of lush greenery is home to the impressive wines of Adeline Wegmüller. Producing around 15,000 bottles annually, Adeline, who spent time working in New Zealand's vineyards, brings an adventurous edge to her expressive reds, memorable whites and a lively sparkling blend of Chasselas and Gamay. Every sip encapsulates her quiet commitment to Swiss viticulture. Before leaving, attempt the garden's challenging labyrinth (below) – perhaps after another glass for courage. Visits by appointment only.

lagara.ch

La Gara's Adeline Wegmüller and (inset) the labyrinth

Three Lakes

Château d'Auvernier

Place des Epancheurs 6,
2012 Auvernier

Train station Auvernier

Rising majestically above the shores of Lake Neuchâtel, Château d'Auvernier is a regal testament to four centuries of winemaking mastery. This grand estate with its weathered stone walls has been in the same family since 1603. In 2022, 15th-generation winemaker Henry Grosjean took the reins. Various tasting offers allow you to step back in time, sampling refined vintages in the château's deep cellars. A key standout is their *Oeil de Perdrix* – an exquisite rosé, pale as dawn, yet bursting with character.

chateau-auvernier.ch

Le Petit Château

Route du Lac 134,
1787 Môtier (Vully)

Train station Sugiez

A gem on the shores of Lake

Château d'Auvernier

Murten. For more than 200 years the Simonet family have tended the vines in this oft-overlooked region north of Lausanne. The winery is open from April to December, with tours available by appointment, and the tasting room is a great spot to sip wine and soak in the views. Their award-winning, biodynamic wines include the rare Freisamer (Freiburger) grape – worth the trip alone. Enhance the visit with one of the historic walks amongst the vines at nearby Mont Vully (see p140).

lepetitchateau.ch

Le Petit Château

Schott Weine
Dorfgasse 47, 2513 Twann

Train station Twann

'The joy of wine is also in the discussion' is the philosophy behind this biodynamic-certified winery near the shores of Lake Biel/Bienne. Since 2016,

energetic winemaker Anne-Claire Schott has been creating dynamic, terroir-rich wines such as Anne-Sombre – a single-plot blend of Gamay, Diolinoir and Gewürztraminer. The former art and sociology student regards her vines as distinct characters, each playing a role in conveying the narrative of the wine – personal and profound. Anne-Claire welcomes small groups to share stories and taste on Friday evenings between 5-7pm and on Saturday mornings. It's best to call ahead.

schottweine.ch

German-speaking Region

aagne weingut
Oberwiesenstrasse 47, 8215 Hallau

Train station Wilchingen-Hallau

Meaning 'own' in the local Schaffhausen dialect, aagne's wines capture the personality of the Klettgau Valley. Winemaker Stefan Gysel creates wines that are both approachable and

Anne-Claire Schott

aagne weingut

intriguing. The new tasting room allows views of their expansive vines and visitors can sample the full range of wines – including their celebrated Blauburgunders and Riesling-Silvaners (see p64, Müller-Thurgau). Local cheese and bread is served alongside. The shop and tasting room are open on Saturdays between 10am and 2pm, no appointment needed.

aagne.ch

Martin Donatsch of Domaine Donatsch

Domaine Donatsch

Sternengasse 6, 7208 Malans

Train station Malans

A true trailblazer, Thomas Donatsch revolutionized winemaking in Switzerland. A rebel *with* a cause, he began planting forbidden varieties, ageing wines in French oak, and launched Switzerland's first traditional-method sparkling wine. His bold vision and refined craftsmanship reshaped the reputation of Malans

and inspired his peers across Switzerland. Thomas passed away in 2024, and his son Martin now carries the torch, producing complex, expressive wines that honour both place and legacy. Tastings are held in the family's 19th-century tavern *Zum Ochsen*, Wednesday to Saturday, 11am to 8pm. Booking essential.

donatsch.info

JET Wein

Kreuzsteinstrasse 35c, 8707 Uetikon am See

Train station Uetikon

Tourism executive turned winemaker Jonas Ettlin has been garnering a good deal of attention since he released his first wines just a few years back. The boutique estate, located at Uetikon, along Lake Zürich, makes approximately 20,000 bottles a year. Jonas hosts regular tasting sessions in

JET Wein

multiple languages at his cellar. Special private events take place at his 'wine hut' deep among the vines, where he pours the wine and runs the barbecue. Make sure to sample his take on Räuschling (see p56), which sold out (twice) at the 2024 Paris Olympics.

jetwein.ch

Weingut Fromm

Baguggiweg 21, 7208 Malans

Train station Malans

Five generations, two continents and a cellar full of stories: the Fromm family's pioneering roots stretch beyond Switzerland to New Zealand, where they helped shape the country's modern wine scene before returning to Graubünden and bringing a worldly edge to the winery. Today, son Marco leads the charge, crafting top-scoring Pinot Noirs and Chardonnays from the dramatic slopes above the village. Tastings are intimate

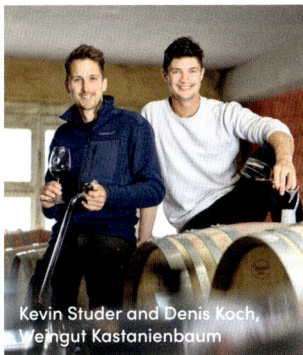

Kevin Studer and Denis Koch, Weingut Kastanienbaum

and insightful, and Marco's small-batch gin makes a playful addition. The recently renovated 17th-century guesthouse offers a perfect excuse to stay the night.

weingut-fromm.ch

Weingut Kastanienbaum

Breitenstrasse 6,
6047 Kastanienbaum, Luzern

Train station Luzern

Named after the chestnut trees that line its grounds, this lakeside estate near Switzerland's legendary birthplace is abuzz with new energy. Since 2022, young winemakers Kevin Studer and Denis Koch have brought fresh ideas to the winery, earning them the title 'Rookie of the Year' from GaultMillau in 2024. Their range includes an award-winning Merlot aged in barrique, alongside more experimental pours matured in concrete eggs

Weingut Fromm

and clay amphorae. The duo welcome guests for tastings Monday to Friday, or by appointment on Saturdays.

weingut-kastanienbaum.ch

Ticino

Fattoria Moncucchetto

Via Crivelli Torricelli 27, 6900 Lugano

Train station Lugano

It's the infectious energy of head winemaker Cristina Monico that makes a visit to this estate so memorable. Since 2009 she has been crafting multi-award-winning wines, including the Moncucchetto Riserva and Refolo Spumante Brut – all expressions of Cristina's deep connection with Ticino. Tastings, held Tuesday-Saturday by appointment, take place in the Mario Botta-designed cantina. The experience culminates at the winery's restaurant, where chef Andrea Muggiano's colourful, seasonal dishes pair joyously with each

Cristina Monico of Fattoria Moncucchetto

Fa'Wino's Simone Favini and Claudio Widmer

pour. Before leaving, be sure to try their classic *Ratafià della Nonna* – grandma's walnut spirit.

moncucchetto.ch

Fa'Wino

Via Borromini 20,
6850 Mendrisio

Train station Mendrisio

The name Fa'Wino fuses the surnames of founders Simone Favini and Claudio Widmer, whose shared vision brought their winemaking project to life. Working small parcels on the slopes of Monte San Giorgio and Monte Generoso, where clay and limestone soils meet long hours of sunshine, they produce fewer than 30,000 bottles annually. Standouts include Saltimbanco sparkling Merlot and Meride Merlot, which is aged in Swiss oak. Tastings can be hosted amongst the vines at Tremona – six wines paired with local cheeses and meats, offering an intimate reflection of the pair's passion and persistence. Prior reservation required.

fawino.ch

Vinattieri

Via Siro E Gianmaria Comi 4,
6853 Ligornetto

Train station Mendrisio

Don't be fooled by Vinattieri's unassuming exterior – inside, a true symphony awaits. Led by the charming sommelier Ramesh Oertli, the *Sinfonia in Rovere* tour is an opus of storytelling and craftsmanship. From the 40m (131ft) long barrel room to the secret vintage library, each stop builds toward a grand crescendo – tasting the top-scoring Vinattieri Rosso and Ligornetto, both elegant expressions of Mendrisiotto's rich vineyards. Available Monday to Friday, bookings essential.

vinattieri.ch

Vinattieri

The best Swiss wine tourism experiences

While winemakers aren't always available to host your visit, local guides, experience providers and tourism offices now offer an ever-expanding menu of wine-centric activities — vineyard hikes, panoramic bike rides, sunset wine cruises, winemaker-hosted lunches aboard vintage trains and even wellness retreats among the vines. Often, the most memorable moments come from the least expected places.

La Vigne Domaine Bovy, Chexbres

The experiences listed here take advantage of almost every mode of transport Switzerland has to offer. In Ascona, you can sip local Merlot while gliding across Lake Maggiore in a classic speedboat. In Lavaux, the whole family can enjoy 360-degree vineyard views aboard the Lavaux Express train. There's Zürich's Dine & Wine Walk, a TukTuk tasting tour in Geneva and even a hot-air balloon ride over the Alps with the Three Lakes Fondue Flight.

This chapter doesn't try to list them all — but it will guide you to a thoughtful selection of unforgettable ways to taste and explore Swiss wine country.

Valais

La Vigne Wine Therapy, Sion (and other locations)

Guérite Sainte-Anne, Route Sainte-Anne, 1950 Sion

This award-winning concept transforms wine into pure wellness with grape-infused soaks, revitalising grape-seed scrubs and Cabernet body wraps; also at two other stunning locations – Château Salavaux in Vully and Domaine Bovy in Chexbres (see p125). Each spa offers vineyard views and a chance to sip the region's finest wines in total relaxation.

la-vigne.ch

Maison de la Petite Arvine

Chemin des Marètsons 1, 1926 Fully

Born in Valais, Petite Arvine – with its bright citrus notes and lick of salinity – has its *de facto* home in Fully. In homage to this grape's remarkable origins (see p55), the new Maison de la Petite Arvine is the first space dedicated entirely to its story. Housed in a former wine cellar, the museum chronicles Arvine's journey through immersive exhibits, artworks, guided walks and (of course) tastings.

maisonpetitesarvines.ch

Visperterminen Vineyard Hike

Balfrinstrasse 3, 3930 Visp

This day out in upper Valais combines history, hiking and Heida (see p60). Start with a

Maison de la Petite Arvine

Visperterminen Vineyard Hike

scenic ascent to Visperterminen, then follow the Beitra bisse – a 600-year-old man-made irrigation channel with sweeping views of the Bietschhorn and Matterhorn. After a hearty lunch, descend to St Jodern Kellerei (see p123) for a guided tasting of local wines and liqueurs. The day ends with a peaceful walk along an educational trail flanked by dry stone walls, leading back to Visp. Operates Monday-Friday, May to October. Bookings must be made online.

valais.ch/en/shop/activities

Vaud

BAM train with La Voie des Sens
Place de la Gare 2, 1110 Morges

Take a sojourn of a different kind aboard the historic BAM

BAM train

Lavaux Express

train. This rail-and-dine experience takes travellers along a scenic route from Morges to Bière, with winemakers joining the journey to share their craft. The three-hour excursion, running Friday to Sunday, includes a seasonal meal paired with wines from a featured producer. The train's bright green carriages – some dating back to 1895 – add vintage charm to this award-winning adventure.

lavoiedessens.ch

Lavaux Express and Lavaux Panoramic

Enjoy 360-degree views of the Lavaux vineyards with the Lavaux Express or Lavaux Panoramic train tours. The Express has two routes departing from Cully and Lutry, while the Panoramic sets off from Chexbres station. This is a family-friendly experience, the open-sided carriages giving panoramic views of ancient châteaux and the historic terraces. Along the way, stop off at local wine cellars and enjoy a glass or two. Bookings advised.

lavauxexpress.ch
lavaux-panoramic.ch

Château d'Aigle
Place du Château 1, 1860 Aigle

Framed by the Alps and rolling vineyards, this fortress with a

Château d'Aigle

view has a serious love for wine. Dating back to the 12th century, the former residence of the Knights of Aigle now houses a world-class vine and wine label museum. Just a short stroll from Aigle's train station, it's a great way to discover the little-known stories of Swiss viticulture – preceded or followed by a tasting at one of the nearby wineries. Open Tuesday to Sunday.

chateauaigle.ch

Walk & Wine
1095 Lutry
Discover Vaud's vineyard regions on foot, tracing Lavaux's cascading terraces or past the storybook châteaux of La Côte. Offered in multiple languages, Walk & Wine's certified heritage guides share stories of winemakers, traditions and local quirks you might miss alone. Suitable for both small and large groups, tailored experiences are available for those looking to venture deeper into the vines. Offered in the summer months, the Lavaux VIP package includes a guided walk, curated tastings and a memorable picnic amidst the vines.

walknwine.net

Wine & Ride
Route Cantonale 9, 1071 Rivaz
An exhilarating two-hour guided

Walk & Wine

Wine & Ride

Fondue Flight

e-bike tour through the heart of Lavaux. Choose from three different routes, operated at different times of the day – the sunset tour is by far the most popular. Suitable for couples to large groups, it brings a new perspective to these renowned vineyards. The tour ends with a tasting of wines at Domaine Chaudet, Titouan Briaux's lakeside estate. Operates 7 days a week, from April to October.

wineandride.com

Geneva

TukTuk Vineyard Tour
Chemin du 23 août-13,
1205 Genève
This enjoyable, open-air ride aboard a classic Thai three-wheeled taxi brings you stunning views from Mont Blanc to the ancient Jura mountains. Along the route, winemakers welcome you with tastings of their artisan wines. If there's a particular winemaker you wish to visit, let them know and the team will help arrange.

welo.swiss

Three Lakes

Fondue Flight
Champ Vionnet 8,
1304 Cossonay
The perfect marriage of fondue and Chasselas, while drifting peacefully above the Alps. This hot air balloon experience launches from stunning

TukTuk Vineyard Tour

Vully Vineyard Walk

Where winemakers dine

What a stunning location. The restaurant **Alter Torkel** sits amidst the vineyards of **Jenins** and has an unobstructed view over the Rhine Valley. This does not mean that Oli Friedrich (GaultMillau Sommelier of the Year 2013) and his team intend to rest on their location laurels. The wine list is absolutely committed to the many fantastic local producers who are the source of their distinguished 'Fine-Wineing' concept. All the dishes, which range from simple to highly refined, match perfectly with a corresponding wine. The Alter Torkel might not be the cheapest spot in the region, but it is absolutely worth a visit. Their occasional hedonistic Sunday-Afternoon parties are truly legendary.

**Marco Fromm,
Weingut Fromm,
Malans, Graubünden**

locations between Gruyères and Lausanne, offering a breathtaking backdrop of snow-covered peaks and shimmering lakes. The 90-minute flight concludes with champagne and Swiss meringues. Offered all year round; in summer the flight takes off to meet the sunset.

ballons-du-leman.ch

Vully Vineyard Walk

Route du Lac 114, 1787 Môtier
Explore the history of Vully, where Roman settlements, WWII secrets and generations of winemaking intersect. Guided by locals in English, French and German, wander on vineyard trails with sweeping views of Lake Murten, Lake Neuchâtel and Mont Vully. Along the way, uncover ancient sites such as the Helvètes ramparts dating back more than 2,000 years. Tours last around 90 minutes and run year-round; advance booking is recommended. A great way to work off a wine tasting, or before an apéro.

tourisme@vully-les-lacs.ch

German-speaking Region

Dine & Wine Hike Stammertal

Humlikonerstrasse 1,
8450 Andelfingen

Just under an hour from central Zürich, this easy hiking trail begins at Stammheim station and winds 13 km (8 miles) through hop fields and vineyards to the hilltop Château Schwandegg before returning. You'll follow well-marked paths and informative panels on grape varieties and winemaking. Tastings await at the Keller estate in Stammheim, Weingut Glesti in Oberstammheim and biodynamic pours at Trottengarten and Schwert. A warm *tarte flambée* – a local speciality – greets you halfway through your journey, and a self-print map card guides every step. Advance booking is required for all tastings.

Dine & Wine Hike

zuercher-weinland.ch/ erlebnisregion/angebote- fuehrungen/weinerlebnisse/

Klettgau Horse-drawn Carriage Tour

Hauptstrasse 50,
8217 Wilchingen

This is a trip aboard a charming horse-drawn carriage, past Pinot Noir vines, pausing for tastings with some of the region's best winemakers. Available over summer, this family-friendly experience – suitable for large groups – is a tribute to the pioneers who first planted Pinot Noir here. The open-topped carriage has a sunshade, and the

Klettgau horse-drawn carriage tour

Ship & Wine at the Rhine Falls

tour can be adapted according to individual needs.

schaffhauserland.ch

Ship & Wine

Dorfstrasse 8,
8212 Nohl am Rheinfall
The mighty Rhine Falls, Europe's largest waterfall, plunges over 20m (65ft) in a roaring spectacle that draws more than a million visitors each year. But few know about the two-hour twilight river cruise that pairs this dramatic backdrop with five local wines and regional cheeses. As you glide past the falls, winemakers share their stories. Seats and dates are limited, so book ahead.

schiffmaendli.ch/en/weinschiff-schaffhausen

Weinkrone Museum

Bergstrasse 3, 8215 Hallau
Near the German border, Hallau's Weinkrone Museum gives an insight into the region's centuries-old

winemaking traditions. Housed in a former vintner's home, it pairs a display of vintage winery tools with a tasting room featuring over 50 wines from 25 local producers. The on-site *Gaststube* serves regional fare, and the village's much-loved bakery is just around the corner. Open on weekends; other times by appointment.

weinkrone.ch

Wine & Water Tour

Im Zogg 7, 7304 Maienfeld
This full-day tour begins in Bad Ragaz with a scenic post-bus ride into the Tamina Gorge and a visit to the *Altes Bad*

Weinkrone Museum

Wine & Water Tour

Aperitivo on the Water

Pfäfers – Switzerland's oldest preserved Baroque bathhouse, dating back to the 12th century. Afterwards, guests enjoy a regional lunch with wine pairing. The afternoon continues in the vineyards of the Bündner Herrschaft, featuring expert-led tastings and insights into the area's viticultural heritage. Available from late April to end of October; non-alcoholic options can be ordered. Suitable for groups of 4-10 people.

wine-tours.ch

Ticino

Aperitivo on the Water

Via Muraccio 142, 6612 Ascona

Glide across the waters of Lake Maggiore aboard a sleek Lido speedboat, glass of Merlot in hand. This experience pairs Ticino's finest wines with artisanal local delicacies – think creamy formaggini and crisp grissini. As the sun dips behind the mountains, the captain navigates secluded coves and islands. Prior reservation required.

castellodelsole.com/en/signature-experiences/

Bike 'n' Wine

Via Sotto Bisio 5, 6828 Balerna

Mendrisiotto Terroir offers guided bicycle tours through the vineyards of the most southern wine region of Switzerland. The 5km (3 mile) route visits family-run wineries such as Cantina Cavallini and Tenuta Montalbano, while the 8 km (5 mile), 5-hour Ginbisbino tour ends with wine and gin tastings along with an evening barbecue. The company stresses that both tours are entirely downhill.

mendrisiottoterroir.ch

Bike 'n' Wine

The best Swiss hotels for wine lovers

Stunning views... luxurious surroundings... Michelin-starred dining... From the quintessential to the downright quirky, Swiss hotels are world-renowned for their hospitality and offer something to suit every pocket.

Badrutt's Palace (see p.xx)

Switzerland does hotels like it does train journeys: precise, epic and with no shortage of panoramic views. Whether you're here to ski, hike, sip or simply slow down, there's a stay to suit every mood – and, contrary to reputation, every budget. Yes, this is one of the most expensive countries in the world. But the range of accommodation is as varied as its mountain peaks.

Of course, you'll find Belle Epoque palaces basking in their lakefront glory and design-led hideaways that feel more like home than hotel – but also stripped-back mountain inns with creaky floorboards and cowbells clanging in the distance. At one end, there are spa hotels serving six-course chef's menus under chandeliers; at the other, family-run lodges dishing out *rösti* and wine poured from a carafe. You'll spend – but you'll spend well.

'Switzerland does hotels like it does train journeys: precise, epic and with no shortage of panoramic views'

For the wine-curious, choosing the right base changes everything. Switzerland's wine regions are scattered and proudly distinct, so proximity matters. Some of the country's most striking stays offer front-row seats to the Swiss wine story: châteaux perched above vines or deluxe hideaways where the cellar deserves as much attention as the spa. Winery stays are relatively few for now, but with some planning, you can experience the very places where the bottles are born – or at least close enough to hear the pop of a fresh cork.

You don't need to be a millionaire or a mountaineer – though both are catered for. From the revered terraces of Lavaux to glacier-framed lodges in Valais, urban boutiques in Zürich and sun-drenched terraces in Ticino, every stay brings a new perspective, another pour – and, inevitably, one more awesome vista.

Chetzeron Hotel

Valais

Chetzeron Hotel & Restaurant $$$
3963 Crans-Montana

At over 2,100m (6,890ft), this four-star retreat – formerly a cable car station – blends natural materials and minimalist design to let the dramatic landscape take centre stage. Two restaurants serve hearty cuisine, with the panoramic dining room a favourite among skiers. The focus is on fresh, local ingredients paired with a wine cellar showcasing leading Valais producers such as Marie-Thérèse Chappaz and Domaine des Muses. And crowning it all: a rooftop pool where mountain vistas stretch on forever.

chetzeron.ch

The Capra $$$$
Lomattenstrasse 6, 3906 Saas-Fee

The Capra is a quiet triumph of Swiss-inspired design and wellness – awarded two Michelin Keys for its thoughtful

The Capra

The Lodge

luxury. The Peak Health Spa is its soul, with hydrotherapy pools, saunas, salt therapy and mountain-facing daybeds. Earthy tones and natural materials carry through the 24 rooms and suites, each a snug retreat. Dining is local and seasonal, from the farm-to-table Brasserie 1809 to panoramic breakfasts at Spielboden, reached by a short cable car ride. Intimate chef-led dinners in the wine cellar can also be arranged.

capra.ch

The Lodge $$$$$
Ch. de Plénadzeu 3, 1936 Verbier

A favourite of celebrities and royals, Richard Branson's luxurious nine-bedroom lodge is a vast, wood-lined chalet just a five-minute walk from town. With a Michelin-trained private chef, outdoor jacuzzi, indoor pool, large games room and staff always ready with a drink from the excellent cellar – or just a slice of homemade cake – it's easy to see why guests find it hard to leave the Lodge's warm embrace. Verbier's slopes are legendary for skiing but the area also shines in summer, with idyllic hikes soundtracked by the customary cowbells.

virginlimitededition.com/the-lodge

Whitepod $$
Les Giettes, Des Cerniers, 1871 Monthey

Above the town of Monthey, in the heart of the Swiss Alps, this eco-luxury retreat offers a unique perspective. The distinctive geodesic pods immerse guests in nature, with panoramic views of Lake Geneva and the vineyards of Chablais

Whitepod

and Valais. Ideal for families, Whitepod combines adventure and relaxation with activities like skiing, hiking, mountain biking and wine tasting.

whitepod.com/en

Vaud

Beau-Rivage Palace $$$$
Chem. de Beau-Rivage 21, 1006 Lausanne

One of Switzerland's most distinguished addresses, the Beau-Rivage Palace boasts a guestbook few can rival: Charlie Chaplin, Coco Chanel and King Hussein have stayed here, adding a touch of glamour to the serene calm of Lake Geneva. Mere steps from Port Ouchy, the Olympic Museum and a short drive to the Lavaux vineyards, it sits at the heart of the Vaud experience. Along with Anne-Sophie Pic's Michelin-awarded restaurant, there are five other

dining options, each with their own comprehensive selection of Swiss wines worth exploring.

brp.ch

Lausanne Palace $$$
Rue du Grand-Chêne 7/9, 1003 Lausanne

In a prime location between city rooftops and the shimmer of the lake, Lausanne Palace blends polished modernity with a thread of historic grandeur. Signature

Beau-Rivage Palace

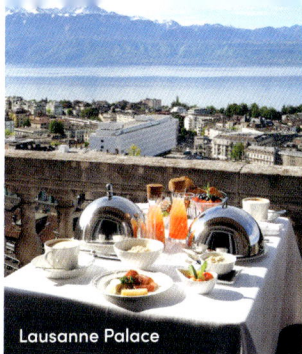
Lausanne Palace

rooms and well-positioned suites offer views over the bustling city centre or the Alps beyond. Downstairs, the multi-awarded La Table (see p152) serves inspired seasonal dishes. The in-house wine bar, an insider favourite, champions Swiss producers with flair, as does the old-world Brasserie du Grand-Chêne.

lausanne-palace.ch

Le Baron Tavernier Hotel & Spa $$
Rte de la Corniche 4, 1070 Puidoux

For those wanting to experience life in the heart of Lavaux's vineyards, this four-star hotel and spa, with its smart, spacious rooms and understated design, has some of the region's most dramatic vistas. Restaurant Le Deck impresses with polished seasonal cuisine paired with wines from nearby Dézaley, Calamin and further afield. If you want to splash out, you can book Lionel Rodriguez's Chef's Table, with inspired four- and six-course options. Given the hotel's elevated setting, arranging transport is recommended for exploring the surrounding wine regions.

barontavernier.ch

Hôtel de Rougemont & Spa $$
Chem. des Palettes 14, 1659 Rougemont

This intimate chalet-style hideaway is all about authentic details – weathered wood, wool

Le Baron Tavernier Hotel & Spa

Hôtel de Rougemont & Spa

Beau-Rivage, Geneva

throws and the soft tones of Alpine stone. Each of the 33 rooms is bathed in natural light, with wide windows framing Vaud's mountain peaks. In the kitchen, chef Andrea Gaia specializes in Mediterranean dishes. For something different, the Wine Room offers groups private Alpine feasting paired with rare vintages.

hotelderougemont.com

Geneva

Beau-Rivage $$$$
Quai du Mont-Blanc 13, 1201 Genève

This is one of Geneva's most famous hotels. Overlooking the Jet d'Eau with Mont Blanc on the horizon, it has welcomed international stars from Elizabeth Taylor to Eleanor Roosevelt. The suites have a fin-de-siècle opulence with swagged curtains and original mouldings

– and most look directly across the lake. Downstairs, Michelin-starred Le Chat-Botté has a cellar with more than 1,500 wines.
beau-rivage.ch

Domaine de Châteauvieux $$$
Chemin de Châteauvieux, Rte de Peney-Dessus 16, 1242 Satigny

The vines surrounding Domaine de Châteauvieux have been here longer than the building itself. The original château burned down in the 16th century. The

Domaine de Châteauvieux

The Woodward $$$$$
Quai Wilson 37, 1201 Genève

This all-suite Michelin-starred hotel distils Geneva luxury into 26 'residences' designed by Pierre-Yves Rochon, dressed in marble and silk and framing lakeside views. There are two restaurants: the late Joël Robuchon's signature L'Atelier (see p165), and the lighter, greener elegance of Le Jardinier. There is a Guerlain spa, but the real indulgence is above – soaking in a tub with Mont Blanc rising in the distance.

aubergeresorts.com/the-woodward/

current property, a mere 500 years old, is now part of the Relais & Châteaux collection, with 13 well-appointed rooms and a celebrated restaurant led by Philippe Chevrier, which has held its Michelin star for over 35 years. The kitchen draws from the château's own herb garden, and diners can choose from a 20,000-bottle wine cellar. The summer terrace offers magical views across the vineyards to the Rhône river and the Jura mountains.

chateauvieux.ch/en

Three Lakes

Hôtel Palafitte $$$
Route des Gouttes d'Or 2, 2000 Neuchâtel

Europe's only five-star hotel on stilts stands above Lake Neuchâtel. Designed in collaboration with German corporate giant Siemens, each

The Woodward and Jet d'Eau

pavilion is a private cocoon with vineyard views and, on clear days, glimpses of both the Eiger and Jungfrau. Days slip by between swims off your own swing ladder, winery tours inland and aperitifs of *Oeil de Perdrix* rosé on the deck. There are three dining concepts to explore, including the Summer Bay terrace and La Table, where chef Ludovic Pigeat fuses French finesse with Asian flair.

palafitte.ch

German-speaking Region

Bad Osterfingen Guest House $$

Zollstrasse 17, 8218 Osterfingen

Hidden away in the wine village

Hôtel Palafitte

of Osterfingen, this lodge was built in 1472 as a summer retreat for the Abbot of Rheinau. Its thick wooden beams and creaking floors echo its past. Today, it welcomes travellers with timber-clad rooms, flickering candlelight and a warm, lived-in charm. No stay is complete without a meal at the in-house restaurant (see p178), where stellar wines, house-cured

Bad Osterfingen Guest House

Badrutt's Palace

meats and seasonal specialities transform a visit into a feast of tradition.

badosterfingen.ch

Badrutt's Palace $$$$
Via Serlas 27, 7500 St. Moritz

Johannes Badrutt turned St Moritz into a winter playground for English tourists in the mid-19th century, and the 155-bedroom palace bearing his name has been welcoming well-heeled guests ever since. With its turrets, high ceilings and stone fireplaces, the hotel retains its fairytale feel. But today, it has several dining options, from a gourmet ice creamery to fondue laced with champagne and truffles, and dining in the former tennis court at La Coupole. Le Grand Hall bar offers views across the Engadin Valley.

badruttspalace.com

Hotel Glacier $$$
Endweg 55, 3818 Grindelwald

This four-star retreat offers wine-centric luxury in the heart of Grindelwald, framed by the dramatic silhouette of the Eiger. The sleek, Alpine-inspired

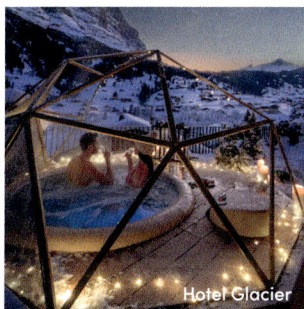

Hotel Glacier

Where winemakers dine

Les Touristes in **Martigny** is a must-visit for lovers of fine dining. Chef duo Maël Gross and Christophe Genetti, friends since childhood, create vibrant menus every week by respecting local and seasonal ingredients. The aesthetics of the dishes are also a feast for the eyes. As for the wines, sommelier Sébastien Vix knows how to find perfect pairings that enhance the pleasure of the whole experience. The wines by the glass change regularly, and here again, the emphasis is on quality and proximity. The decor is refined, but the atmosphere remains relaxed and warm. I have never been disappointed coming here.

Mathilde Roux,
Cave de l'Orlaya,
Fully, Valais

design creates an immersive retreat, with signature rooms boasting private outdoor pools for uninterrupted mountain views. The new Cork Club spotlights Swiss wine, from *Mémoire des Vins Suisses* rarities to unexpected finds, while curated wine dinners range from vertical tastings of Pontet-Canet to sparkling 50-house champagne flights. A place for those who seek the stories behind the glass.

theglacier.ch/hotel-glacier/

Iglu-Dorf, Gstaad (also Zermatt and Davos/Klosters) $$

Saanerslochgrat, 3776 Saanen

Rebuilt each winter from scratch, this igloo village is a fleeting Alpine world carved entirely from snow and ice. Find the snow walls etched with intricate motifs, a glowing bar sculpted from a single block of ice, and beds of compact

Iglu-Dorf

Les Trois Rois

snow topped with faux fur and thermal layers. Soak under the stars in a wood-fired hot tub before indulging in a steaming pot of fondue. Come morning, enjoy breakfast at altitude before the descent, with the option to ski, snowshoe or travel via cable car.

iglu-dorf.com/en/locations/

Les Trois Rois $$$$
Blumenrain 8, 4001 Basel

Where the Rhine flows past Basel's old town, this historic hotel has been welcoming the great and curious since 1681. Napoleon stayed here, as did Queen Elizabeth II. But it's not just the portraits that impress. The staff excel at making guests feel part of the hotel's living history – though the riverfront views are a close second. Start with a glass of regional wine at the old-world bar (see p189),

then settle in for Michelin-level dining at Peter Knogl's Cheval Blanc. For a more casual vibe, hearty French and Swiss classics or afternoon tea are served in the brasserie.

lestroisrois.com/en/

Park Hotel Vitznau $$$$$
Seestrasse 18, 6354 Vitznau

A fairytale castle along the shores of Lake Luzern, this architectural beauty blends understated luxury with a rich sense of history. Built on three

Park Hotel Vitznau

pillars – Art & Culture, Wine & Dine and Health & Wealth – each suite tells its own story, inspired by a famous person, place or institution. Exquisite materials like Bulgarian limestone exude an air of sophistication as does Focus Atelier, the two-Michelin-starred dining concept. The wine list is a true highlight, with six cellars holding more than 40,000 bottles (the oldest dating back to 1795).

parkhotel-vitznau.ch

Park Hyatt Zurich $$$$
Beethovenstrasse 21, 8002 Zürich

Located in the heart of Zürich, just steps from the famed Bahnhofstrasse, the Park Hyatt epitomizes understated luxury. Its sleek yet inviting design blends warm earthy tones with floor-to-ceiling windows that radiate the energy of this cosmopolitan city.

A big drawcard is parkhuus, where an open kitchen meets a mesmerizing glass-framed wine library housing more than

Park Hyatt Zurich

3,000 bottles. Nearby, Zürich's lakeside vineyards beckon for a tasting tour, which staff can help organize. Service is warm and attentive yet discreet.

hyatt.com/en-US/hotel/ switzerland/park-hyatt-zurich/

Schlaf-Fass, Jenins (also Maienfeld) $
Unterdorf 14, 7307 Jenins

A giant wine barrel for a bedroom – surely every wine lover's dream after a day of degustation. In the heart of Graubünden's Heidiland region, two sites have repurposed 8,000-litre barrels to create cozy sleeping pods. Dining takes place in the neighbouring barrel, and bathroom facilities are not far away. Set among rolling vineyards, this wine-themed escape is quirky and unfiltered. Available year-round.

schlaf-fass.ch

Schlaf-Fass

The Dolder Grand $$$$$
Kurhausstrasse 65, 8032 Zürich

Above Zürich, where forest meets sky, this five-star

The Dolder Grand

residence is less a hotel than a world unto itself, where gastronomy takes the lead. Its historic turrets and modern wings house serene rooms, panoramic terraces and an award-winning spa of near-mythical reputation. But it's the culinary offering that truly excites: The Restaurant by Heiko Nieder (2 Michelin stars, 19 GaultMillau points) serves intricate tasting menus and a remarkable wine list spotlighting the best of Swiss vintners. Saltz brings bold design and classic comfort; Mikuyara fuses Japan and Peru; and Blooms is quietly

radical with its vegan and vegetarian garden fare.

thedoldergrand.com

Ticino

Villa Castagnola $$$
Via Pico 9, 6900 Lugano

Like the pages of a storybook, this welcoming retreat whispers tales of its distinguished past. Once a noble residence, the property is filled with precious antiques and museum-worthy artwork that catch the eye at every turn. Guests can unwind in the spa, sip wine on the Lido lakeside terrace or enjoy gourmet cuisine at award-winning Galleria Arté al Lago, La Rucola and Le Relais – which offers a creative vegan tasting menu and wine pairing option. Practise some *dolce far niente* – the art of doing nothing – in the lush subtropical garden, a stone's throw from Lake Lugano and Alpine vistas.

villacastagnola.com

Relais Castello di Morcote $$
Portich da Sura 18, 6921 Vico Morcote

Where ancient tales and contemporary design intertwine, this castle hotel offers an intimate escape wrapped in centuries-old stone and vineyard air. Its 12 rooms blend restored

Villa Castagnola

timber, soft textiles and Asian design notes, bringing both flourish and quiet confidence. The Gianini family estate invites guests to taste organic wines at Tenuta Castello di Morcote, among the most respected in Ticino. The nearby Restaurant Vicania, set in a rustic farmhouse with mountain views, serves unfussy seasonal fare and wine pairings. Mornings begin at La Sorgente beneath a vine-laced pergola, where the lake glints just beyond your teacup.

relaiscastellodimorcote.ch

Relais Castello di Morcote

Fine dining in Switzerland

Switzerland doesn't often make a foodie's bucket list. People come for the peaks, the pistes – perhaps a pot of fondue. And yet, quietly and without fuss, this landlocked country has crafted one of Europe's most alluring dining scenes. It's the sentinel of quality: season-led menus, produce with provenance and chefs – many locally trained – who cook with a sense of place and a spark of imagination.

Arakel (see p164)

Switzerland consistently ranks among the world's top five countries for Michelin-starred restaurants. You wouldn't know it, because these kitchens don't shout about it. They just do it. From Restaurant de l'Hôtel de Ville in Crissier, and Tanja Grandits's poetic plates at Stücki, to forest-fringed discoveries like Flora and Stefan Beer's Radius in Interlaken, a quiet confidence runs through them all. The bread isn't bad either.

Many share addresses with some of the country's most renowned hotels – IGNIV at Grand Resort Bad Ragaz, La Table at Lausanne Palace – where deep cellars and generous wine budgets allow sommeliers to showcase rare vintages and lesser-known Swiss producers. Wine is no afterthought here; it's a narrative thread running through the meal.

Forget the fondue clichés. This is fine dining at its peak – refined, revered, and a little unexpected.

Valais

La Table du Vingt-deux
Route des Creux 22, 1936 Verbier

Maxime Gombaud's secret restaurant calls itself a speakeasy, and access is hidden inside wine and cocktail bar Le Crock No Name. But speakeasies don't generally offer six-course tasting menus, or wind up in the Michelin Guide. Whatever you call it, this tiny venue has become one of Verbier's most sought-after dining addresses: finely tuned combinations of local ingredients and international influences, a mouthwatering French and Swiss wine list and a relaxed yet knowing ambience may be the justification for that speakeasy label. Bookings essential.

crock.ch/en

La Table du Vingt-deux

Restaurant Au 1465, Au Club Alpin

Route du Lac 21,
1938 Champex-Lac

High above Martigny and the steep vineyards of Valais, chef Mariano Buda – barely 30 years old – unleashes a fearless culinary vision. At Au 1465 (relating to its altitude), he transforms Alpine ingredients into vivid, sculptural plates that echo the wild beauty outside: Alpine suckling pig done three ways or marbled beef fillet in puff pastry with pistachio and mountain flowers. The dining room is sleek but grounded – stone, wood and glass framing lake and peak views like a still life. With rare finds from the Cave du 1465's vast cellar, this is where mountains, innovation and wine collide in thrilling harmony. Open Wednesday to Sunday.

auclubalpin.ch/en/restaurant-bar

Restaurant Au 1465

Vaud

La Table, Lausanne Palace

Rue du Grand-Chêne 7/9,
1003 Lausanne

When Franck Pelux and Sarah Benahmed took over the restaurant in 2019, they transformed Lausanne Palace's culinary identity and quickly won their first Michelin star in 2021, followed by a second star in 2024. Gone is the Riviera flair; in its place, an intimate, velvet-toned room. Dishes arrive

La Table, Lausanne Palace

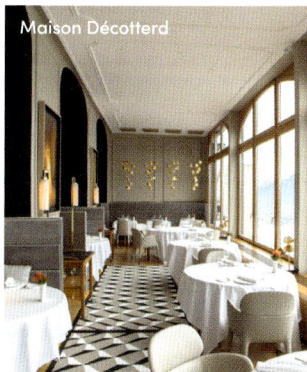

Maison Décotterd

sculptural yet seasonal, marrying Pelux's techniques with Alpine nuance, such as his gnocchi with forest morels resting on a cloud of mountain herbs. A wide selection of Swiss wines tie the entire experience together. Sarah's intuitive, gracious service softens the formality. Her smile alone lights up the room. Open Wednesday to Saturday for lunch and dinner.

lausanne-palace.ch/restaurants-bars/la-table-du-lausanne-palace/le-restaurant

Franck Pelux and Sarah Benahmed

Maison Décotterd

Route de Glion 111, 1823 Glion

An elevated dining experience, chef Stéphane Décotterd's commitment to regional, sustainable cuisine shines throughout – an elegant tribute to the Léman region and his Swiss heritage. Set within one of Switzerland's premier hospitality schools, the space combines modern refinement with a welcoming atmosphere, offering both a fine-dining restaurant and a relaxed bistro-bar. The wine list is exceptional, highlighting the chef's personal favourites and rare local finds. Standout dishes include crayfish from Lac de Joux with verbena, and pink rhubarb ravioli with coltsfoot flowers by award-winning pastry chef Christophe Loeffel.

maisondecotterd.com/

Restaurant de l'Hôtel de Ville

Restaurant de l'Hôtel de Ville, Crissier

Rue d'Yverdon 1, 1023 Crissier

An icon in Swiss dining, Crissier's three-Michelin-starred institution continues to astonish under chef Franck Giovannini. Dishes like ice cubes of Bernese rose tomatoes with pata negra or féra vitello from Lake Geneva with caper flowers and glacier nectar showcase his precision and imagination. The wine list is a tome full of diverse, rare and intriguing selections from across Switzerland. Be prepared to be swept away. Book well in advance.

restaurantcrissier.com

Geneva

Arakel

Rue Henri-Blanvalet 17, 1207 Geneva

Michelin-starred Arakel feels like an urban secret. The zinc-

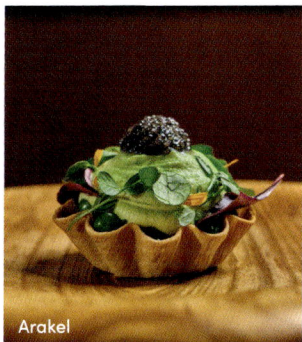
Arakel

L'Atelier Robuchon
Quai Wilson 37, 1201 Geneva

Protégé of the legendary Joël Robuchon, chef Olivier Jean crafts an immersive dining experience built on flavour, finesse and colour. Set within the ultra-luxurious Woodward Hotel (see p151), this Michelin-starred gem seduces the senses – deep red hues, sleek wood tones and the intoxicating aroma of French-Asian fusion shaped by Olivier's time in China. At the 36-seat counter, watch the culinary artistry unfold: dishes such as wild monkfish roasted with herbs served with a yellow curry sabayon and sea asparagus, or a moreish coconut and raspberry mousse with lemongrass sorbet. For the ultimate indulgence, opt for the tasting menu with wine pairing.

aubergeresorts.com/the-woodward/dine/latelier-robuchon/

topped bar leads into a low-lit dining room that frames the open kitchen. Chef Quentin Philippe and his team craft expressive, modern dishes like saffron-laced mussel risotto or wild shrimp carpaccio with yuzu. The awarded wine list is equally compelling, with over 50 Swiss labels including rare vintages from Neuchâtel's Maison Carrée. Elegant and relaxed. Closed weekends.

arakel.ch

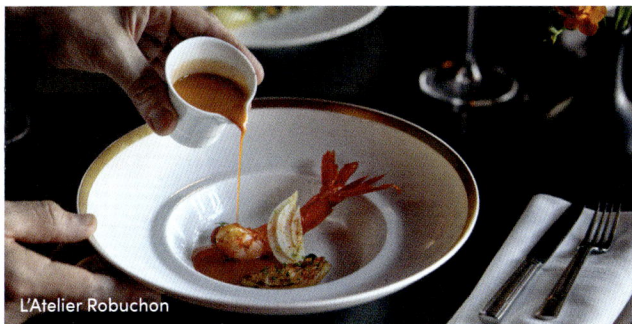
L'Atelier Robuchon

Three Lakes

Flora
Chez Sémon 1, 2714 Le Prédame

A passion project from partner-chefs Davina Comment and Matthias Waser, Flora is a soulful new hideaway tucked into a reimagined woodland farmhouse in Canton Jura. Its seasonal tasting menus reflect both emotion and sustainability, shifting regularly with local harvests and producers – trout with fennel and saffron, or lamb with chard and black garlic. Wines are thoughtfully sourced from small Swiss producers, with a strong local focus. Sundays bring a regionally inspired brunch, making it as much a destination as a delicious detour through the forests of the Franches-Montagnes.

florarestaurant.ch

Flora

fine-dining sharing experience. The ever-changing menu, led by chef Joël Ellenberger, celebrates local produce with a flair for modern flavours. An expansive wine selection, including rare magnums, continues the narrative of sharing. Spanish designer Patricia Urquiola's interior completes the homely ambience: warm and welcoming.

resortragaz.ch/igniv

KLE
Zweierstrasse 114, 8003 Zürich

Chef Zineb 'Zizi' Hattab brings her Moroccan-Spanish heritage

German-Speaking Region

IGNIV, Grand Resort Bad Ragaz
Bernhard-Simonstrasse 14, 7310 Bad Ragaz

Born from the mind of three-Michelin-star chef and TV personality Andreas Caminada, IGNIV – meaning 'nest' in the local Romansh language – invites guests to a unique

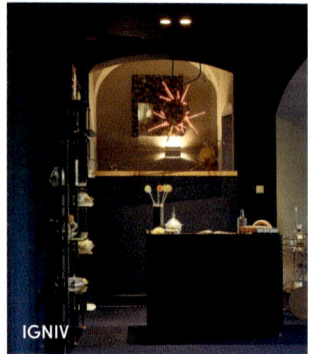

IGNIV

Zizi Hattab, KLE

and Michelin-honed craft to the table, creating vibrant, plant-based dishes that burst with character. The space leans industrial-chic and hums with energy, reflecting KLE's mission of sustainability and innovation. With an ever-evolving menu – available in four, five or six-course surprise formats – and natural or biodynamic wine pairings, the experience feels fresh, modern and deeply personal.

restaurantkle.com

Stücki, Basel
Bruderholzallee 42, 4059 Basel

Tanja Grandits runs her kitchen with masterful precision. At her Michelin-starred, 19-point GaultMillau restaurant in Basel, she fuses Swiss roots with global influences to create dishes that are vibrant, balanced and quietly daring – like ricotta buns infused with passion fruit honey and sweet potato relish, or mountain lentils in pistachio beurre blanc with bay leaf and lettuce. The wine list is just as thoughtful, featuring expressive

Stücki

Swiss references such as Alex Stauffer's Cornalin 'L'O de l'A' and Completer by Roman Hermann.

tanjagrandits.ch

Radius, Victoria Jungfrau Hotel
Höheweg 41, 3800 Interlaken

Under the gaze of the mighty Jungfrau, Radius by Stefan Beer takes the 'local for local' ethos seriously. Every ingredient is sourced within a 50 km (30 mile) radius – no olive oil, no pepper, just Alpine ingenuity. Even the butter is made locally, and the bread is baked with ancient grains from fields near the hotel. Expect dishes like veal tongue with lake perch and capers, or arctic char with celery and fermented carrot. Vegan set menus and sharing plates ensure variety. A destination restaurant with true terroir on the plate.

victoria-jungfrau.ch/restaurants-bars/radius-by-stefan-beer/

Ticino
La Brezza, Hotel Eden Roc
Via Albarelle 16, 6612 Ascona

Framed by the glimmering Lake Maggiore, La Brezza offers a dining experience where mountains meet the Mediterranean. Guided by chef

Radius

Marco Campanella's precise, flavour-driven cooking, dishes such as Iberico pork cheek with Jerusalem artichoke, or Sambirano chocolate from Madagascar with sea buckthorn and cocoa fruit juice, showcase regional identity and inventive, technique-led pairings. For a more holistic option, the Moving Mountains menu is entirely plant-based, crafted with foraged Alpine ingredients, complex sugars and gut-friendly grains designed to nourish as much as delight. The sommelier pairing experience brings intention and allure to any menu. The setting is intimate and modern, nestled within the luxurious Hotel Eden Roc.

tschuggencollection.ch/en/
hotel/hotel-eden-roc

La Brezza

Casual dining in Switzerland

If Swiss fine dining is precise and poetic, casual dining is its quieter twin – less dressed up, but just as self-assured. You don't come here for bargain bites. Even modest bistros can feel like they're flirting with fine dining. But what you do get are small rooms, compact menus and fewer covers. Many places are family-owned and operated. No PR machine – just people who know exactly what they're doing.

Osteria Castello-Sasso Corbaro (see p183)

There's an ease to it all – an unspoken belief that good food doesn't need fuss to make it memorable. From a plate of *rösti* to a hearty banquet of venison with wine poured from a carafe – when it's good, it's very good.

Town and country

And the best meals aren't confined to cities. Some of Switzerland's most remote villages serve up its most memorable dining – Grotto Sassello, hidden in Ticino's Verzasca Valley, or Bad Osterfingen, on the fringes of the Black Forest. Some venues are only reachable on foot – or skis. Think grilled perch in a chalet with glacier views, or beef tartare on a lakeside terrace, and yes, plenty of cheese.

Swiss casual dining today is confident, authentic and deeply rooted in place. It just so happens that many of those places come with views as mouthwatering as the food.

Valais

Brasserie Uno $$$
Kirchstrasse 38, 3920 Zermatt

A relaxed but inventive dining experience. Luis Romo and Tommaso Guardascione's six-course surprise tasting menu showcases star dishes like pike-perch with creamed sauerkraut and Swiss caviar – a vegan-friendly option is also available. The interior is the pair's take on rustic-chic, adorned with personal mementos complementing the seasonal, sustainable cuisine. With one Michelin Star, one Green Star and 15 GaultMillau points, it's a compelling culinary destination in the heart of Zermatt.

brasserieuno.com

Brasserie Uno

Le Partage, Aïda Hôtel & Spa $$$$
Chemin du Béthania 1, 3963 Crans-Montana

Avid skier and restaurateur Franck Reynaud's third concept

is for those who love to share. Set in an elegant adults-only hotel, diners choose from 10 or 15 ever-changing tasting portions, drawing on Italian-inspired flavours and local ingredients; think trout cannelloni with tarragon and roasted leeks. Wines come from nearby producers, personally selected by Franck. The warm, wood-rich interior is matched by polished service and a view that might just convince you to book an extra night. Closed April-July.

aidahotelspa.ch/en/restaurant-bar

Raclett'house Chez Eddy $$
Route de Valbord 55, 1934 Bruson

Eddy Baillifard is a true master of cheese. Among his many accolades, he set a world record in 2025 for hosting the largest raclette event – uniting 5,000 cheese lovers in one molten celebration. He created this mountain retreat as a kind of

Chez Eddy

pilgrimage for raclette devotees. Inside, it's all golden, bubbling perfection served with flair in a rustic dining room. Valais wines flow freely, perfectly paired with the cheesy house speciality. Open year-round, evenings fill up fast – especially in winter – so book ahead. Cozy accommodation is available upstairs.

eddy-baillifard.com

Vaud

Alpine chalet Le Vermeilley $$
Vermeilley, 1273 Arzier-Le Muids

Known as the *Palais des Fondues*, this remote winter chalet is reached via an easy, appetite-inducing, hike from La Givrine train station. Complete with open fire and communal tables, you will soon feel at home and ready to indulge in more than 20 different fondues prepared by the young and welcoming team. A favourite is the chèvre and wild garlic. Wash it all down

Le Partage

Alpine chalet Le Vermeilley

with wines from the La Côte area. Lunch is first come, first served. For dinner, book well in advance. Cash only.

levermeilley.com

Auberge de la Gare $$
Rue de la Gare 1,
1091 Grandvaux

An institution since 1862, the Auberge offers a convivial atmosphere with panoramic views only minutes from the vineyards and Grandvaux station. The wine list is personally selected by the chef and shows off the best of Lavaux. Pair the house-classic beef tartare with Plant Robert.

aubergegrandvaux.ch

Auberge de la Gare

L'Appart $$$$
Rue de Bourg 29,
1003 Lausanne

A refreshing addition to Lausanne's dining scene. L'Appart is led by chef Luis Zuzarte and manager Nicolas Bernier, who transformed a former pizzeria into a quietly ambitious space for immersive, flavour-driven dining. Seasonal dishes are thoughtful and inventive – think local whitefish with tomato, pollen and hazelnuts, or pasture-fed pork shoulder with braised romaine, apricot and sprouted wheat. Wine flights curated by Bernier highlight small producers – like the work of Sandrine Caloz in Valais, or exclusive offerings

Nicolas and Luis of L'Appart

from Lionel and Aude at Cave du Signal in La Côte. For a more personal experience, book the chef's high table. A subtle but elegant detail: the names of the service team are printed on the daily menu.

appart-lausanne.ch

Les Trois Sifflets $$
Rue du Simplon 1, 1800 Vevey

At the 'Three Whistles', devour delicious fondue (made to a secret recipe) and Lavaux wines, served with a sizable portion of patriotic pride. The jovial staff, kitted out in military regalia, deliver each steaming pot of cheese to the blare of *Marche du Général Guisan*. Post-meal, pose for a photo dressed up in various Swiss costumes. Immersive, spirited revelry – and a super-sized peppermill.

Call: +41 021 921 14 13

Les Trois Sifflets

The view from Ze Fork

Ze Fork $$$
Rue du Léman 2, 1800 Vevey

At one of the most scenic spots along the shores of Lake Geneva, this contemporary bistro and bar serves up modern classics with an emphasis on local provenance. The site of an old printing factory, it has been under the management of mother and son duo Christine and Jean Bodivit since 2012. Inside, exposed lake stone and panelled ceilings hark back to its industrial past. The outdoor terrace, very busy in the summer months, is the perfect vantage point for beautiful sunsets.

zefork.ch

Geneva

Café des Banques $$$
Rue de Hesse 6, 1204 Geneva

A modern eatery behind a discreet façade in Geneva's banking quarter. Chef Yoann Caloué – awarded 15/20 by GaultMillau – delivers dishes

Café des Banques

such as langoustine with rhubarb and lobster remoulade, accompanied by a wine list featuring mainly local and French wines. The Chartreuse soufflé is justly celebrated.

cafedesbanques.com

Gallo $$$

Boulevard du Pont-d'Arve 26, 1205 Geneva

On this buzzing Geneva boulevard, Gallo pulses with energy – and so does its lively chef, Jacopo Romagnoli, who brings bistro classics to life: 60-day aged Swiss Angus with prime gravy, or hand-dived scallops cooked over charcoal. The room hums with rhythm, warmth and the clink of wine glasses. It's a place to settle in, get a little messy and eat well.

gallogeneve.com

Ottolenghi, Mandarin Oriental Hotel $$$

Quai Turrettini 1, 1201 Geneva

Yotam Ottolenghi's first international outpost brings his vibrant Mediterranean cuisine to Geneva. Inspired by his London restaurant ROVI, the menu highlights open-flame cooking, fermentation and local provenance – think smoked carrot escabeche or grilled cabbage with sunflower tahini. The Swiss wine list stands out,

Gallo

Ottolenghi, Mandarin Oriental Hotel

with references sourced from across the various regions. Classic brunch offerings are already a hit, served in a bright, mural-filled space mere steps from the Rhône.

mandarinoriental.com/en/geneva/rhone-river/dine/ottolenghi

Three Lakes

Brasserie du Poisson $$
Rue des Epancheurs 1, 2012 Auvernier

Overlooking the shimmering waters of Lake Neuchâtel, this brasserie serves up fresh, local seafood in a relaxed atmosphere. Whether it's the tender perch fillets or the famous fish soup, each dish is expertly crafted to showcase the best of the region's bounty. And no reason to halt the wine journey, with a menu of Neuchâtel's finest wines to keep you hooked.

lepoisson-auvernier.ch

Ecluse $$$

Schüsspromenade 14D,
2502 Biel/Bienne

At this intimate riverside
brasserie, chef Simon Künzli and
his team work with a hyper-
local ethos – every seasonal
ingredient is sourced within
50 km (31 miles). The result
is a menu of inventive, waste-
conscious dishes such as baby
fennel 'dragonfly' with peanuts
and candied wild garlic, or
the popular cherry tarte tatin,
served with fior di latte ice
cream and honey from their own
bees. The wine list focuses on
local and some key European
organic producers. There's a
strong showing of Swiss pét-
nats that pair beautifully with
the restaurant's light, precise
cooking.

ecluse-biel.ch

Ecluse

German-speaking Region

Bad Osterfingen $$$

Zollstrasse 17, 8218 Osterfingen

Stepping through the doors
of this historic gem – dating
back to 1472 – you can almost
hear the echoes of its former
guests. Now run by the Meyer
family, the popular restaurant
celebrates Swiss culinary classics
with a contemporary touch. The
estate's terroir-driven wines,

Brasserie du Poisson

Bad Osterfingen

including the highly acclaimed 'Badreben Abt' and 'Zwaa' sparkling, are rich in character and history – stories the staff are eager to share. With on-site accommodation (see p152), guests can stay longer, soaking in the timeless winemaking heritage of Osterfingen.

badosterfingen.ch

Blaue Ente $$$
Seefeldstrasse 223, 8008 Zürich

Under the guidance of Alexandre Hannemann since 2024, this laid-back eatery reimagines local flavours with seasonal twists – their speciality is duck. But the true showstopper is the top-tier wine list, named Switzerland's best by *Falstaff* magazine in 2025, which brims with regional gems: Orange Riesling-Silvaner by Jonas Ettlin (see p130), 'Ottoberg' Müller-Thurgau by Michael Broger and a non-filtered Chasselas from Château d'Auvernier (see p128) are just a few.

muehle-tiefenbrunnen.ch/blaue-ente

Glou Glou $$
Waldstätterstrasse 7, 6003 Luzern

Glou Glou might sound like baby talk, but Luzern locals know it

Blaue Ente

Glou Glou

ever-changing selection of world-cuisine small plates inspired by the chef's travels – from Japan and beyond. Imagine zucchini cassoulet with bamboo shoot emulsion, or US Prime short rib curry doused with persimmon vinaigrette and truffle. Thoughtful pairings spotlight Swiss wines – from crisp Adank Brut to Petite Arvine Vieilles Vignes from Histoire d'Enfer (see p61). The team also serve their 'Easy Lunch' and Sunday brunch at their original Steinhalle restaurant in the Old Town (17 GaultMillau points).

myle-bern.com, steinhalle.ch

as the go-to spot for some of the city's best beef tartare – and if that's not your thing, try the perch and caviar with barbecue sauce and fine herbs. The vibe is playful yet polished, with a brunch-to-dinner menu as relaxed as the smiling staff who serve it. Recognized by Star Wine List, the wine selection leans local with standout natural styles. Great for groups, it feels like a neighbourhood hangout crossed with your coolest friend's dinner party.

glouglou-luzern.ch

MYLE $$$$
Bubenbergpl. 5A, 3011 Bern

MYLE, at Bern station, has been reborn under Markus Arnold's casual-dining team, featuring a sleek show kitchen, walk-in wine cellar, and an

Markus Arnold at MYLE

Restaurant Wunderbrunnen $$$

Dorfstrasse 36, 8152 Opfikon

Owner Roger Hirzel opened Wunderbrunnen partly to house his 40,000-bottle collection and partly to share the kind of wines most people never get the chance to taste. The smart, seasonal menu draws on Mediterranean and Asian influences, like the salmon tartare with sakura and sour cream. Each dish is designed to complement a wine list that includes 700 Swiss labels, several older vintages and over 120 by-the-glass options. Roger, a sommelier and member of *Mémoire des Vins Suisses,* focuses on thoughtful pairings. Closed on Sunday.

wunderbrunnen–opfikon.ch

Wine cellar, Restaurant Wunderbrunnen

Schloss Maienfeld

Schloss Maienfeld $$$

Schloss Maienfeld 2, 7304 Maienfeld

This sprawling 13th-century estate located in the heart of Graubünden's emblematic Heidiland region (see p44) has been beautifully restored and reimagined as a foodie's destination. Within the castle stone walls, you'll now find a restaurant, bistro, *vinothèque* and a bar-lounge that pairs rustic elegance with contemporary style. The seasonal menu honours Alpine flavours with standout dry-aged meats, while the wine list teems with Bündner Herrschaft producers. Don't skip the finale: a signature Irish Coffee, flamed and finished at your table.

schlossmaienfeld.ch

Ticino

Badalucci $$$$
Via Cassarate 3, 6900 Lugano

Chef Marco Badalucci brings a painter's touch to the plate, using seafood as his medium. His southern Italian roots and fine-tuned European training shine through in seasonal dishes like millefeuille of sea bass and foie gras with artichoke salad and balsamic reduction, or the seared scallops with cardamom apple cream and local mortadella. The setting is modern, the service intuitive and the wine list deep, with strong representation from Ticino and Graubünden. Open Tuesday-Saturday, it's a highlight of Lugano's evolving food scene.

badalucci.com

Badalucci

Grotto Sassello

Where winemakers dine

Masseria Cuntitt in **Castel San Pietro** is one of my go-to restaurants in the largest winegrowing commune in Ticino, near Mendrisiotto at the southernmost tip of Switzerland. This casual-elegant restaurant occupies a beautiful Lombard-style farmhouse in the delightful historic centre of the small village. The young chef, Federico Palladino, and his attentive, friendly staff develop dishes with authentic and deep flavours, combining innovation with tradition. Federico pays great attention to the quality of produce, seeking to enhance the excellence that the Ticino region has to offer. A must-try is the carbonara with local guanciale and Sbrinz cheese mousse. Great importance is also attached to the selection of wines, and two charming terraces provide the perfect setting for alfresco dining in summer.

**Alfred De Martin,
Gialdi Vini SA,
Mendrisio, Ticino**

Osteria Castello-Sasso Corbaro $$
Via Sasso Corbaro 44,
6500 Bellinzona

High above Bellinzona's rooftops, this hidden trattoria sits within the castle walls of the highest of the town's three UNESCO-listed fortresses. After a morning exploring the iconic towers, reward yourself with a meal in the courtyard, traced with grapevines and stories of old. The menu leans Mediterranean with a strong Ticinese soul – risotto, lake fish and vibrant antipasti. Also perfect for a lazy afternoon aperitivo. Open Wednesday to Sunday.

osteriasassocorbaro.ch

Grotto Sassello $$
Permaioo, 6635 Gerra (Verzasca)

Grotto Sassello is a quiet ode to Ticino's grotto dining tradition. Set beneath chestnut trees in

Osteria Castello-Sasso Corbaro

the wild beauty of the Verzasca Valley, the menu honours the region: home-cured meats, trout from the valley, goat cheese with dandelion pesto and polenta-dusted plates that speak of the land. The wine list is modest but local, and the tiramisù, whispered about, lingers long after the last spoonful. Flavourful moments to revel in the joy of Ticinese hospitality.

Call: +41 091 746 13 10

The best Swiss wine bars

Surprisingly, for a country so in love with all things vinous, wine bars are a relatively new phenomenon in Switzerland. But for the wine-curious traveller, there are a handful of places where the wine lists dazzle and the atmosphere makes it well worth ordering a glass – or a bottle.

Château de Villa

Switzerland has always run on its own terms – and its wine bars are no different. For decades, the *carnotzet* – cozy cellar nooks where locals gathered for a few glasses and the odd nibble – did the job just fine. Why bother with a menu when your neighbour makes the wine? Sampling bottles from another region, let alone another country, was bordering on radical.

But things are changing. Swiss wines now contend with an increasing demand for international bottles. Entrepreneurial hosts inspired by a new generation of curious drinkers are shaping something bolder: wine bars that champion local producers while casting their nets a little wider. You can now sip a Geneva Gamay in Zürich or a Completer in Lausanne – no train ticket required.

The pace of change is patchy. Some regions, such as Ticino, still favour a spritz over a glass of local Merlot. Others, like Valais, stay fiercely loyal – wines from elsewhere remain rare. But for the intrepid, the scene is rewarding and diverse: urban spots with captivating wine lists, lakeside lounges with well-stocked cellars and unassuming counters where Swiss wines get the spotlight they deserve.

Valais

Château de Villa

Rue Sainte-Catherine 4, 3960 Sierre/Siders

This local favourite offers a chance to immerse in Valais' tastes and traditions. At the Sensorama, you'll learn to identify the nuanced aromas and textures of top regional wines. And with more than 650 bottles from over 100 producers – 20 rotating by the glass – you're spoilt for choice. The casual restaurant's signature quintet of raclette is a must, along with the house fondue, air-dried meats and an autumn staple: *brisolée*. Open daily.

chateaudevilla.ch

Elsie's Wine and Champagne Bar

Kirchpl. 16, 3920 Zermatt

Tucked inside a traditional chalet on Zermatt's main street, Elsie's offers a warm welcome and rustic wood interiors. The extensive wine list has something for everyone but pays tribute to Swiss terroir, with standout pours from Domaine Chevaliers

Elsie's Wine and Champagne Bar

in Salgesch and the audacious Salix Chenin Blanc by Domaine Louis Bovard (see p104). Settle in with a tasting platter at the bar or linger longer over dinner in the cozy dining room.

elsiesbar.ch

Vaud

Domaine de la Crausaz
Chemin de la Creuse 9, 1091 Grandvaux

This is a bar experience with a view few can match. Run by winemaker Maxime Dizerens, the historic estate – owned by the family since 1515 – offers breathtaking views paired with his full range of wines, from vintage Chasselas to lesser-known Sauvignon Blanc and Plant Robert (see p62). Small sharing plates complement every glass, and from April to November the team offers a Sunday wine brunch concept,

where visitors can sample a buffet of cheeses, meats, breads and other delicious local fare.

lacrausaz.ch

Le Poisson Rouge
Rue des Deux-Marchés 24, 1800 Vevey

Netting a table here in the evening is no easy feat – and for good reason. This lively wine bar is a fresh addition to Vevey's scene, drawing locals with its expertly curated wine list featuring pours from across Switzerland and beyond. Each month brings new by-the-glass selections, paired with well-crafted tapas and sharing platters. A true hot spot to sip something new while indulging in wine-centric conversation.

lepoissonrouge.ch

Le Poisson Rouge

Maison des Vins de La Côte
Route du Coeur de la Cote 1, 1185 Mont-sur-Rolle

This new offering above the town of Rolle blends the rich culture of the region's wine heritage with a contemporary bar that is pleasing to both the eye and the palate. Managed by Nathalie Ravet, a former GaultMillau Sommelier of the Year and sister of multi-awarded chef Guy Ravet (see p158), the Maison provides a space to enjoy the wines of more than 80 La Côte producers from 40 different grape varieties. And it's definitely a family affair: father Bernard, also an award-winning chef, helps out in the kitchen along with Nathalie's mother and sister, crafting immaculate sharing platters.

maisondesvins.ch

Domaine de la Crausaz

Maison des Vins de La Côte

Geneva

Chez Bacchus

Cr de Rive 7, 1204 Geneva

It's no surprise the God of wine has found favour here, in one of Geneva's most happening neighbourhoods. Don't let the simple interior fool you – there's a lot to take in, with more than 40 wines available by the glass daily. There's a particular focus on Geneva producers, like Jean-Pierre Pellegrin and Domaine de la Vigne Blanche (see p126) and estates like Weingut Obrecht in Graubünden. The team also runs regional theme nights for more committed oenophiles. All bottles are available for purchase in their shop.

caveaudebacchus.ch

Tablard

Rue Saint-Joseph 26,
1227 Carouge

This cozy yet vibrant haven is where wine (and cheese) lovers hang out. Located in the funky suburb of Carouge, it boasts a regularly revolving selection of Swiss and international wines. These are paired with artisanal cheeses – from next door's Fromagerie De Bleu! – and tapas prepared by Galician chef Mariano Lopez. The upbeat staff know their wines and can recommend something to suit any mood. Don't miss the cheese cellar, visible through a glass portal in the floor.

tablard.ch

Tablard

Oenothèque Chauffage Compris

Three Lakes

Oenothèque Chauffage Compris
Rue des Moulins 37,
2000 Neuchâtel

This snug haven promises a warm reception for wine aficionados. And you'd be forgiven for asking where to begin, with more than 250 wines by the glass – the majority of them Swiss. Inside, large communal tables set the scene for sampling, while a few outdoor seats offer a breezier spot for a balmy tasting. A range of daily *apéro* platters completes the experience.

oenotheque.chauffagecompris.ch

German-speaking Region

Bar Les Trois Rois
Blumenrain 8, 4001 Basel

Swiss wine is the focus at this buzzing Basel institution. Located within the luxury hotel of the same name, it attracts wine lovers with its biodynamic options and little-known gems from small wineries across Switzerland – nearly a dozen are local producers. The open fire is a magnet in cooler months, but it's hard to resist the summer terrace with views over the Rhine. Winner of Swiss Bar of the Year, open daily until midnight.

lestroisrois.com/en/restaurants-bars

Chez Smith
Grubenstrasse 27, 8045 Zürich

Just outside the city centre, this bar and bistro attracts a diverse crowd in search of great wine and food any day of the week. With an award-winning cellar boasting over 1,000 wines – many Swiss, including rare finds like Petit Meslier by Tom Litwan in Aargau or a Zürich sparkling from HerterWein – there's plenty

Bar Les Trois Rois

Auberge de la Clef d'Or
in **Bursinel** is a traditional regional inn, but with one big plus: I love taking my family there. The owners and their staff are all incredibly kind and friendly. You will find classic regional dishes and well-prepared meats. The restaurant serves unpretentious yet ambitious French cuisine. The more the years go by, the better they get. The best evidence is their entry into GaultMillau last year with a 13 rating. The wine list is almost exclusively regional – which I rather like – with a varied and high-quality selection of wines by the glass. The team knows each producer well, as they visit them regularly.

**Vincent Graenicher,
Domaine de Penloup,
Tartegnin, Vaud**

Chez Smith

to intrigue. If in doubt, the staff are knowledgeable and keen to offer pairing suggestions. The interior blends modern chic with an industrial edge, while a deli counter and outdoor terrace add to its charm. A top spot for both small and large groups.

chez–smith.ch

Stall 247

Spitalgasse 16, 7304 Maienfeld

Housed in a former cowshed, just a yodel's distance from 'Heididorf' (see p44), this popular bar serves up a bountiful selection of wines from the Bündner Herrschaft area paired with seasonal locally sourced tapas and platters. It

Stall 247

Widder Bar

has a rustic, lived-in charm and Mirco Hug and Christof Gisler know how to rouse guests with regular events. Where cows once roamed, now wine lovers gather. There's also a vinoteca, so you can buy local wines to take away.

stall247.ch

Widder Bar, Widder Hotel

Widdergasse 6, 8001 Zürich

Blending modern elegance and an extensive drinks list, this is one of Zürich's best-known bars. With ancient wooden beams juxtaposed against sleek, contemporary panache, it offers cozy sophistication. Likewise, the wine selection is thoughtfully executed, catering to both novices and connoisseurs; many are available by the glass, such as the Chardonnay from Ticino's Cantina alla Maggia and the Vieilles Vignes Pinot Noir by Jacques Tatasciore in Neuchâtel. There are live jazz performances as well.

widderhotel.com/en/eat-drink/widder-bar/

Ticino

Bar La Fontana

Via Ai Monti della Trinità 44, 6600 Locarno

Slip through the doors of Hotel Belvedere and straight into Bar La Fontana – Locarno's go-to for serious wine drinkers. The list runs deep, with plenty from Ticino, plus Swiss regional rarities worth lingering over. Pair a glass with a plate from the connected restaurant, where Mediterranean flavours meld with local, sustainable ingredients. When the weather is fine, the garden terrace seals the deal.

lafontana-locarno.com

Bar La Fontana

The best Swiss wine shops

Most Swiss buy direct from their local producer, but there are some excellent wine shops around the country, both regional specialists and major chains like Mövenpick and Manor, and the comprehensive online specialist Flaschenpost.

Mövenpick Wein (see pp198–199)

Most Swiss wine producers work on such a small scale that many of their best wines are often limited to 5,000 bottles – or fewer. As a result, they are not widely distributed even within Switzerland. The wine shops in this list typically stock between 20 and 40 Swiss producers from most, if not all, of the country's wine regions. Also, there is not much duplication between the different shops, so it's always worth checking their websites (mostly in French or German) to see which estates and wines they stock – especially if you are looking for any of the recommended wines in this book (see p55-77).

Several of the shops are located away from the bigger cities, so either a car is needed or it might be easier to order online if you are staying long enough to receive the delivery. The shop managers and their staff have close relationships with the producers and are keen to share their knowledge.

Suisse Romande

C.A.V.E. SA
Rue de Malagny 28,
1196 Gland

The *Club des Amateurs des Vins Exquis* is exactly that: a club for lovers of exquisite wines. Fortunately, it is open to non-members who can choose from a selection of over 40 producers from across Switzerland and beyond. Its founder, the highly regarded Jacques Perrin, strives to find producers and wines that reflect the place they come from and deliver a memorable sensory experience. The warehouse shop in Gland (between Geneva and Lausanne) has knowledgeable, friendly staff and also sells a limited selection of quality food products and accessories.

cavesa.ch

Carton Rouge
Route de la Gare 44,
1305 Penthalaz

François Gauthier has continued to grow the business created almost 30 years ago by his wine talent-spotting uncle Pierre Müller, listing an extensive range of more than 40 Swiss producers in a new state-of-the-art cellar just north of Lausanne. The well-balanced Switzerland

C.A.V.E. SA

François Gauthier, Carton Rouge

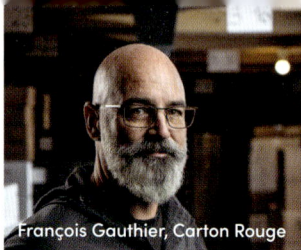

list features wines not just from his home region of Vaud, but from each wine region, with a focus on organic and biodynamic producers. The rest of the list includes an impressive number of producers from almost every region of France.

cartonrouge-sa.ch

Caveau de Bacchus

Cr de Rive 5,
1204 Geneva [also in Gland and Gstaad]

An enthusiastic team of sommeliers makes it a pleasure to shop at these premium wine stores. The original shop is conveniently located in central Geneva, and there are branches in Gland and Gstaad. They carry a broad range of producers from Geneva as well as Valais, Vaud and the German-speaking Region, but only a limited selection from Ticino. On most

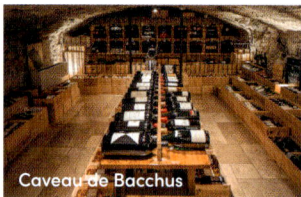

Caveau de Bacchus

Le Passeur de Vin

weekdays the Geneva branch extends into a wine bar and restaurant, Chez Bacchus (see p188), which offers a choice of 40 wines by the glass and a list of 800 wines.

caveaudebacchus.ch

Le Passeur de Vin
25 rue Eugène-Marziano, 1227 Geneva [also in Geneva (Eaux-Vives), Lausanne and Zürich]

Organic, biodynamic and natural wines play an important role at Le Passeur de Vin. Evidence of this is the lunar calendar on its homepage, highlighting fruit, flower, root and leaf days, and describing their wines as 'pure living products'. The selection features more than 25 Swiss producers, mainly from Valais, Vaud and Geneva, and includes a mix of renowned and lesser-known estates. There is also a strong range from neighbouring France as well as diverse sake offerings. In Geneva, the larger shop is away from the centre, while the smaller branch in Eaux-Vives is more easily accessed down by the lake.

lepasseurdevin.ch

Others
Le Naturiste, Fribourg
30+ Swiss producers

lenaturiste.ch

Cantina del Mulino, Fribourg
20+ Swiss producers

cantinadelmulino.ch

German-speaking Region

Smith & Smith
Grubenstrasse 27, 8045 Zürich [other branches in Zürich and Bern]

A little over 10 years ago, Markus Lichtenstein launched his contemporary wine store concept; he now runs several shops in Zürich and Bern. Each one has a young and dynamic

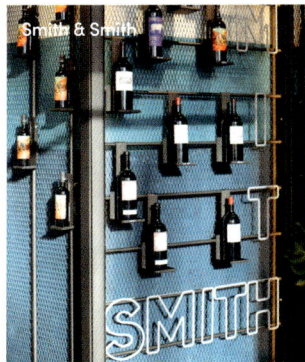
Smith & Smith

look and feel, with staff to match. The Switzerland list represents each region and it's a fascinating range of wines which encourages exploration. The rest of the world is equally well covered. Organic, biodynamic and natural wines are commonplace at Smith & Smith. The Europaallee store at Bridge, the new food and drink hub in central Zürich, doubles as a wine bar.

smithandsmith.ch

Carl Studer Vinothek

Langensandstrasse 7,
6005 Luzern

Manager Roger Janz greets customers warmly to this quality-conscious store, not far from the centre of town. The Switzerland list covers every region of the country (except Vaud) and has a particularly strong representation from Ticino. While the number of Swiss producers may appear limited, each one is recognized as a leading name in its respective region and the wines are highly sought after. Carl Studer also carries wines from six other countries in Europe, as well as

a particularly interesting and eclectic range from California and Washington State.

studer-vinothek.ch

Gerstl Weinselektionen

Sandäckerstrasse 10,
8957 Spreitenbach (near Baden) [also Sempach (near Luzern) and partner shops in Rheineck (near St Gallen), Winterthur, Luzern, Sissach and Laufen (both near Basel)]

Gerstl stocks more than 60 Swiss producers, including several of the top names in each region. The list shows strength and depth in the German-speaking Region, especially Graubünden, as well as an extensive range from the rest of the world. The shops only hold a limited number of wines, so it is worth checking the full list on the website (only in German). To help you discover Swiss wines there are themed compilations in cases of six at special prices. Gerstl operates two stores of its own and works with several partner wine shops in the German-speaking Region, which carry part of their wine

Carl Studer Vinothek

Gerstl Weinselektionen

Baur au Lac Vins

list. Many of them are located away from the main city centres so a car is advisable.

gerstl.ch

Baur au Lac Vins
ShopVille Hauptbahnhof
Bahnhofplatz, 1 8001 Zürich
[also four other stores around
Zürich and Lake Zürich]

This Zürich chain is connected to the city's legendary Baur au Lac hotel, whose reputation for expertise in fine wines and spirits goes back to 1844. While there is a branch just steps from the hotel, visit this one in the underground shopping mall at the main station. They offer a well-curated selection of over 20 leading Swiss producers as well as hundreds of top producers from more than a dozen other countries. Whether you're a wine lover or just curious, the relaxed yet refined wine shopping experience is rooted in the same tradition of quality that has made the hotel world-famous.

bauraulacvins.ch

Others
Vinothek Brancaia, Zürich +
Lenzerheide
40+ Swiss producers
vinothek-brancaia.ch

Martel AG, Zürich + St Gallen
30+ Swiss producers
martel.ch

Le Passeur de Vin, Zürich
(see also **Suisse Romande**)
25+ Swiss producers
lepasseurdevin.ch

Studio Wino (natural
wines), Zürich
20+ Swiss producers
studiowino.ch

Schubi Weine, Luzern
40+ Swiss producers
schubiweine.ch

Ticino
Arvino
Via Emilio Bossi 1
6900 Lugano [also Melano and
Zürich]

These luxury stores invite you to indulge in the world of wine, and the qualified staff will help you to discover suitable wines to

Arvino

match your preferences. There is a strong selection of top Ticino producers and wines as well as leading names from some of the other Swiss regions. The owners have dealt in fine and rare wines for three decades and provide a range of customized services to their clients who collect the very best names in wine.

https://arvi.ch/en/

Others

Casa del Vino, Lugano + Zürich and Zürich area
20+ Swiss producers
casadelvino.ch

Nationwide

Mövenpick Wein (Vins/ Vini)

Soon after World War II, Mövenpick opened its first restaurants in Switzerland. The wines being served proved so popular that it decided to start selling them in dedicated wine stores. 75 years on, it is the only specialist wine retailer nationwide and manages a chain of about 40 stores across the country. In view of the number of stores, it does well to stock a sizeable range of Swiss producers, which includes the Staatskellerei Zürich acquired by Mövenpick in 1997. The list of wines from the rest of the world is equally extensive. In Zürich the Mövenpick Wein-Bar, within

Mövenpick Wein

to laying down for future enjoyment. Food pairing is made easy as there is a wide choice of fresh foods and top brands available all under the same roof.

manor.ch/fr/shop/vin/c/wine

easy walking distance of the main train station, is a popular destination for wine lovers.

moevenpick-wein.com/fr/

Manor

This premium department store brand is present all over Switzerland; 25 of its 56 stores have a Manor Food store-within-a-store featuring a specialist wine department. In each one there is a trained sommelier ready to give help and advice, which makes Manor a real destination for wine lovers. The Swiss selection is extensive, covering each of the wine regions and offering wines that range from everyday drinking

Flaschenpost

The name, which best translates as 'bottles by post', is the clue to this e-commerce business. Flaschenpost was launched in 2007 by two university students, who spotted that wine was missing out on the internet revolution that was changing shopping habits. They created a user-friendly online portal that let shoppers choose from an initial range of 2,000 wines sourced from a dozen wine shops. Flaschenpost now offers a choice of over 30,000 wines from a much bigger number of suppliers. The current catalogue includes over 2,000 Swiss wines from more than 100 Swiss producers. This largest online wine retailer in Switzerland is true to its simple credo: 'We want to make it as easy as possible to buy wine.'

flaschenpost.ch/en

Others
Globus

Department stores with wine departments in seven cities; 30+ Swiss producers

globus.ch/fr/vin-delicatessa/

Wine Advisor at Manor

Glossary

.CH The country URL '.ch' is short for *Confoederatio Helvetica*, Latin for the Swiss Confederation. It reflects Switzerland's multilingual, neutral identity.

Acidity Contributes freshness, balance and ageing potential in wine. It affects flavour, stability and colour, especially in red wines, and is essential to a wine's structure and overall quality.

Alte Reben/Vieilles Vignes Meaning 'old vines' in German/French, it typically indicates vines over 35 years old, though the term is not legally defined. Older vines often produce lower yields but with more concentrated, complex fruit.

AOC (*Appellation d'Origine Contrôlée*) The classification granted by each canton to certain wines based on geographical location and adherence to prescribed traditional practices.

AOP (*Appellation d'Origine Protégée*) A Swiss quality label awarded to products like Gruyère and Alpkäse, made entirely within a defined region using traditional methods. It guarantees the product's origin, authentic craftsmanship and adherence to strict local production standards.

Barrel A cylindrical, often oak container used primarily to age wine. The oak comes mainly from France. Barrels influence flavour and come in various sizes. Unlike larger vats, they are movable.

Biodynamic A holistic farming philosophy based on Rudolf Steiner's principles, using organic methods plus lunar cycles, herbal preparations and a closed ecosystem. Wines often certified by Demeter.

Bisse A historic open irrigation channel used in Alpine vineyards and pastures, particularly in Valais. Dating to the 13th century it is often accompanied by a scenic hiking path.

Cantine Aperte Italian for 'open cellars', this annual event invites the public into wineries across Ticino so they can taste wines, meet winemakers and explore the vineyards.

Canton/Kanton/Cantone Switzerland is a confederation made up of 26 cantons – semi-autonomous states with their own laws, cultures and wine traditions.

Capite A small vineyard shelter, often used to store tools or offer rest and shade. Found across Lavaux in canton Vaud, many are centuries old and now part of the landscape's cultural identity.

Carnotzet A traditional Swiss wine cellar room used for informal gatherings, tastings and meals. Usually found in private homes or wineries, it embodies Swiss conviviality.

Caves Ouvertes French for 'open cellars', this is a popular spring and summer event in Suisse Romande. Dozens of wineries open their doors for tastings, often with food and music.

Cépage French for grape variety.

Climate Switzerland has a wide range of climates in terms of sunlight, rainfall and temperatures, moderated by lakes and Alpine altitude. The diversity of microclimates – often within a single vineyard – is key to the character of its wines.

DOC (*Denominazione di Origine Controllata*) Italian for 'controlled designation of origin', DOC is the equivalent of AOC in Italian-speaking Switzerland. The classification guarantees geographic origin and adherence to strict rules.

Deutschschweiz The German-speaking Region, one of Switzerland's six wine regions, comprising 16 cantons.

Flétri French for 'withered' or 'dried', used to describe grapes left to shrivel naturally on the vine or after harvest to produce concentrated sweet wines.

GaultMillau A respected European restaurant and wine guide. It scores venues up to 20 points or 'hats'. It plays a key role in recognizing top Swiss culinary, hospitality and wine talent.

Grand Cru A premium Swiss wine classification regulated locally, not nationally. At least 90% of grapes must come from the named Grand Cru area, and wines must meet higher ripeness standards and pass annual tasting panels.

Guérite A seasonal vineyard hut or pop-up bar found in canton Valais, usually open in warmer months. Often family-run, it serves simple food and estate wines with panoramic views.

Mémoire des Vins Suisses An exclusive association of Swiss winegrowers dedicated to preserving age-worthy wines. Member estates contribute annually to a central wine library known as The Treasury.

Noble rot Another name for *Botrytis Cinerea*, a beneficial fungus that dehydrates grapes and concentrates their sugars and flavours, which is crucial in the production of sweet wines.

Offene Weinkeller German for 'open wine cellars', typically held in spring in the German-speaking Region. A festive chance to visit producers, taste wines and explore local traditions.

Organic Production of wine according to organic farming principles prohibiting the use of synthetic pesticides, herbicides, fungicides and fertilizers. Wines often certified by Bio-Suisse.

Phylloxera A tiny, root-feeding insect, native to North America, that devastated European vineyards in the 19th century by killing grapevines. It led to the widespread grafting of European vines onto resistant American rootstocks.

Premier Cru A local appellation used only in Geneva for wines of superior quality. The region recognizes 22 Premier Cru appellations which are often tied to specific vineyard sites.

Premier Grand Cru A designation used in Vaud for top wines that meet strict tasting, production and origin standards. It applies to individual wines rather than estates.

Rebe German for vine. 'Rebsorte' means grape variety.

Réserve A widely used but mostly unregulated term implying a higher-quality wine. It can mean anything – or nothing – depending on the producer.

Röstigraben The so-called 'hash browns divide' between German- and French-speaking areas. More than just language, it's where fondue forks meet Bratwurst. Not a physical trench but a cultural fault line the Swiss feel in their bones.

Servagnin A rare and historic red grape variety considered the ancestor of Pinot Noir in Switzerland. Grown exclusively around Morges in Vaud by some 12 estates, under strict AOC rules.

Suisse Romande The French-speaking region of Switzerland comprising cantons Geneva, Jura, Neuchâtel, Vaud and parts of cantons Bern, Fribourg and Valais.

Tannins Natural compounds found in grape skins, seeds and stems, as well as oak barrels, that create an astringent sensation in wine and play a key role in structure, ageing potential and mouthfeel.

Terravin A quality guarantee for wines that are evaluated on a range of at least 20 sensory attributes by a panel of wine experts each year.

Terroir A French term describing the unique combination of natural and cultural factors – such as soil, climate, and local practices – that influence the character and quality of wine from a specific place.

Vin des glaciers An oxidative Alpine wine aged using the solera method in shared old barrels. Now made largely with Marsanne instead of the traditional Rèze variety.

English	French	German	Italian	Romansh
Hello	Bonjour	Grüezi	Ciao **or** Buongiorno	Allegra
Thank you	Merci	Danke **or** Merci	Grazie	Grazia
Cheers	Santé	Proscht **or** zum Wohl	Cin cin **or** Salute	Viva
Enjoy your meal	Bon appétit	En Guete	Buon appetito	Bun appetit
Goodbye	Au revoir	Adieu **or** uf Widerluege	Arrivederci	A revair

Further reading

Swiss wine and food

Swiss Grapes: History and Origin, Dr José Vouillamoz, independently published 2020
> José is a Swiss grape geneticist of international fame and one of the world's leading authorities on the origin and parentage of grape varieties through DNA profiling.

The Landscape of Swiss Wine: A wine-lover's tour of Switzerland, Sue Style, Bergli 2019
> Explores how vine cultivation has shaped the Swiss landscape down the centuries and introduces the reader to Switzerland's best winemakers.

Wine Hiking Switzerland: Explore the Landscape of Swiss Wines, Ellen Wallace, Helvetiq 2023
> Fifty hikes following routes chosen for their beauty through Switzerland's leading wine regions. Every one ends with a visit to an excellent Swiss winemaker.

Helvetic Kitchen: Swiss Cooking, Andie Pilot, Bergli 2023
> Born in Canada to a Swiss mother, Andie started the website Helvetic Kitchen so she could share her love of simple Swiss cooking with her friends.

Essential Switzerland

Swiss Watching: Inside the Land of Milk and Money, Diccon Bewes, John Murray Business 2018
> Proves that there's more to Switzerland than banks and skis, francs and cheese, by dispelling the myths and unravelling the true meaning of being Swiss.

Swissness in a Nutshell, Gianni Haver and Mix & Remix, Bergli 2014
> Illuminates this Alpine nation with cartoons and more – from William Tell to Heidi, Swiss Army Knives to cheese, litter-free streets to punctual trains.

The Indispensable Illustrated Dictionary to Swiss German, Bergli 2022
> Features more than 3,000 of the most important words of Switzerland's most-spoken dialect – as well as some of the most entertaining and misunderstood.

Geography, nature & outdoors

Mountains of the Mind, Robert Macfarlane, Granta Books 2023
> The most exhilarating history of mountaineering. Includes chapters on the Alps and the birth of alpinism.

The Alps: A Human History from Hannibal to Heidi and Beyond, Stephen O'Shea, W. W. Norton & Company 2017
> How the Alps have influenced culture from *Frankenstein* to *Heidi* and *The Sound of Music*; visits the spot of Sherlock Holmes's 'death' scene and more.

The Rhine: Following Europe's Greatest River from Amsterdam to the Alps, Ben Coates, Nicholas Brealey Publishing 2019

Explores the impact that the Rhine has had on European culture and history and explains how influences have flowed along and across the river.

Switzerland in Tolkien's Middle-Earth, Martin S. Monsch, Martin S. Monsch 2021
Describes how Tolkien's 1911 trip through the Swiss Alps, particularly the Bernese Oberland and Valais, served as a significant source of inspiration for his landscapes and narratives.

Famous fiction set in Switzerland

Heidi, Johanna Spyri, Fresh Green Mind Publishing 2024
Classic Swiss novel that gives a sense of Alpine culture. A story about the healing power of nature, city versus country life, and the importance of family and friendship.

Frankenstein, Mary Shelley, Penguin Classics 2003
Written during a poor summer in Geneva when Shelley was 18. It was the winner of a ghost story contest suggested by Lord Byron. Part of Switzerland's literary mythos.

Hotel du Lac, Anita Brookner, Penguin 2023
Her best novel is set in a luxury hotel, out of season, against the backdrop of Lake Geneva and the mountains in French Switzerland. Booker Prize winner 1984.

Doctor Fischer of Geneva or The Bomb Party, Graham Greene, Vintage Classics 2019
A dark satire focused on the wealthy and their insatiable greed. A misanthropic millionaire, known for his lavish parties, tests the limits of his guests' avarice.

The Prisoner of Chillon (annotated), Lord Byron, CreateSpace Independent Publishing Platform 2016
The famous 392-line narrative poem about a man imprisoned for his political beliefs. Written by Byron in 1816 in Ouchy, Lausanne, after a visit to the castle.

Well-known Swiss historical figures

Henry Dunant: The Founder of the Red Cross, Corinne Chaponnière, Bloomsbury Academic 2022
A detailed biography of the Swiss humanitarian who established the International Red Cross and won the first Nobel Peace Prize.

Albert Einstein: A Biography, Albrecht Fölsing, Penguin 1998
Though born in Germany, Einstein became a Swiss citizen in 1901 and developed many of his key theories while working at the Swiss Patent Office in Bern.

Le Corbusier: A Life, Nicholas Fox Weber, Knopf 2008
An acclaimed biography of the Swiss-born architect who transformed modern architecture and urban design.

Carl Jung: Wounded Healer of the Soul, Claire Dunne, Watkins Publishing 2015
Chronicles the life of the Swiss psychiatrist whose theories reshaped modern psychology and who influenced and was influenced by Sigmund Freud.

Index

Acknowledgements

The publishers have made every effort to trace the copyright holders of the text and images reproduced in this book. If, however, you believe that any work has been incorrectly credited or used without permission, please contact us immediately and we will endeavour to rectify the situation. Images of businesses are assumed to be copyright of those businesses.

1 Beat Mueller/Switzerland Tourism, 4 Marc Checkley, Lavaux Classic, 5 Silvano Zeiter/ Switzerland Tourism, Badrutt's Palace Hotel, 6 Vittore Photography/Adobe Stock, 10-11 Domaine Jean-René Germanier 12-14 Wikipedia Commons, 14 Office des Vins Vaudois, 15-17 Wikipedia Commons, 18-19 Jan Geerk/Switzerland Tourism, 20 Shutterstock, 21 Martin Zemlicka/Dreamstime, 22-23 Jan Geerk/Switzerland Tourism, 23 André Meier/Switzerland Tourism, 24-25 Adobe Stock, 25 Jan Schick/Wikipedia Commons, 26 AlpinaVina/J-F Genoud, 27 Gornergrat Bahn, 28 David Carlier/Valais Promotion, 29 AlpinaVina/J-F Genoud, 30 AlpinaVina/ J-F Genoud, 31 Marc Checkley, 32-33 Chlodvig/Dreamstime, 33 Office des Vins Vaudois, 34-35 Office des Vins Vaudois, 34 Jan Geerk/Switzerland Tourism, 35 Christelle Petremand/Office des Vins Vaudois, 35 Office des Vins Vaudois, 37 Régis Colombo/Genève Tourisme, 38 Loris von Siebenthal/Genève Tourisme, 38-39 Alexandre & Dimitri Colomb/Up to you, 40 AlpinaVina/J-F Genoud, 41 Deutschschweizer Wein, 42 Zürich Tourism, 43-45 Deutschschweizer Wein, 46 Gaby Gianini/Swiss Wine, 47 Adobe Stock, 48 Simon Hardy, 50 Deutschschweizer Wein, 52 Vinattieri, 54 Domaine Blaise Duboux, 57 Domaine Donatsch, 56 Wikipedia Commons, 58-59 Christian Hofmann/Switzerland Tourism, 61 Schlossgut Bachtobel, 66 Domaine Donatsch, 74-75 Adobe Stock, 77 Domaine Vitis Musicalis, Neuchâtel Vins et Terroir, 78 Switzerland Tourism, 79 Cully Jazz, 80 Adobe Stock, 80 Divinum, 81 Championnat du monde des tracassets, 81 Weingut Wegelin, 82 Vineria dei Mir, 82-83 Lavaux Classic, 83 Jean-Louis Bolomey, 84 Nina & Kathy Photography, 85 Karen del Zio, 86 Hallauer Herbstfest, 85 Théo Bender/Fully Tourism, 87 Expovina, 87 Bern Tourism, 88 André Meier/Switzerland tourism, 89 Vins Valais, Marc Checkley, 90 Régis Colombo, Swiss Wine, 91 Cantina Mendrisio, 94 André Meier/Switzerland Tourism, 95 Jan Geerk/Switzerland Tourism, 96-114 (maps) Cosmographics, 115 Silvano Zeiter/ Switzerland Tourism, 120 Domaine Jean-René Germanier, 122 Les Celliers de Sion, 122 Marc Checkley, 123 Provins, 123 St Jodern Kellerei, 124 Artisans Vignerons d'Yvorne, 125 Graenicher Vins, 126 Marc Checkley, Brigitte Besson, 127 Patrick Eaton, La Gara, 128 Rawkingphoto.ch, 129 Marco Lopez, 130 Marc Checkley, Domaine Donatsch, 131 Weingut Kastanienbaum, 132 Studiopagi, 133 Fa'Wino, Vinattieri, 134 Elena Schmid/Switzerland Tourism, 135 Petites Arvines Fully, 136 Studiopagi, Vins Valais, FH Solution SARL, 137 Lavaux Express, 138 Andreas Girth/ Switzerland Tourism, Joana Ferreira/Lavaux Patrimoine mondial, Laurent Licari, 139 Ballons du Leman, Welo, 140 Freiburger Tourismusverband, 141 Zuercher Weinland, Schaffhauserland Tourismus, 142 schiffmaendli.ch, 143 Heidiland Tourismus, 143 The Living Circle, 144 Badrutt's Palace Hotel, 146 The Capra, 148 Whitepod Original, 148 Thomas Buchwalder, 149 Lausanne Palace, 150 Guillaume Cottancin, 150-151 www.gauvin.pictures, 152 Schaffhauserland Tourismus, 153 Badrutt's Palace Hotel, 154 Hiepler Brunier, 154 iglu-dorf.com, 155 Grand Hotel Les Trois Rois, 155 Park Hotel Vitznau, 156 Micheles Photographie/Schlaff Fass, 157 Dolder Hotel AG, 158 Villa Castagnola, 159 Egle Berruti, 160 Guillaume Cottancin, 163 Anthony Demierre/Grandes Tables Suisses, 164 Domaine Mermoud, Restaurant de Ville de Crissier, 165 Olivier Mauhin, 166 Grand Resort Bad Ragaz, 167 Nora Dal Cero/hellozurich.ch, DigitaleMassarbeit, 168 Marc Ducrest, 169 Tina Sturzenegger, 170 Fortezza Bellinzona, 171 David Murray, 172 Eddy Baillifard, 173 Marc Checkley, L'Appart, 174 Lee Sze Chuin, Simon Hardy, 175 Guillaume Cottancin, Domino Soko/Florencial Rena, 176 Mandarin Oriental Geneva, 177 Ecluse, 178 Monika Gerber, 179 Floid AG, Rockservice AG, Restaurant Steinhalle, 180 Wunderbrunnen Betriebs AG, 181 Ristorante Badalucci, 183 Fortezza Bellinzona, 184 Château de Villa, 186 Elsie's Wine and Champagne Bar, 187 Domaine de la Crausaz, Le Poisson Rouge, 188 Maison des Vins de la Côte, quandestcequonmange.ch, 189 Marc Checkley, Grand Hotel Les Trois Rois, 190 Ricardo Moreira, Marc Checkley, 191 The Living Circle, La Fontana Ristorante & Bar, 192 Mövenpick Wein, 193 Claude Bernhard, 194 Hans-Peter Siffert, 194 François Wavre, Pawww, 196 Gerstl Weinselektionen, 197 Baur au Lac Vins, 199 Mövenpick Wein, 199 Manor

The authors would also like to extend their thanks to Jérôme Aké-Béda, AlpinaVina.com, Gilles Besse, Blaise Duboux, Jean-François Genoud, Lavaux Patrimoine mondial (LPm), Lisa Ride and Franziska Werren.